VOLKSWAGEN BEETLE

HOW TO BUILD & MODIFY

Eric LeClair and Susan Anderson

S-A DESIGN

CarTech®

CarTech®

CarTech®, Inc.
838 Lake Street South
Forest Lake, MN 55025
Phone: 651-277-1200 or 800-551-4754
Fax: 651-277-1203
www.cartechbooks.com

Edit by Wes Eisenschenk
Layout by Connie DeFlorin

ISBN 978-1-61325-547-6
Item No. SA486

Library of Congress Cataloging-in-Publication Data

Names: LeClair, Eric, 1966- author. | Anderson, Susan, 1968- author.
Title: Volkswagen Beetle : how to build & modify / Eric LeClair, Susan Anderson.
Description: Forest Lake, MN : CarTech, Inc., [2021] | "Item no. SA486."
Identifiers: LCCN 2021058707 | ISBN 9781613255476 (paperback)
Subjects: LCSH: Volkswagen Beetle automobile–Maintenance and repair–Handbooks, manuals, etc. | Volkswagen automo-biles–Customizing–Handbooks, manuals, etc.
Classification: LCC TL215.V6 L433 2021 | DDC 629.28/722–dc23
LC record available at https://lccn.loc.gov/2021058707

Written, edited, and designed in the U.S.A.
Printed in China
10 9 8 7 6 5 4 3 2 1

CarTech books may be purchased at a discounted rate in bulk for resale, events, corporate gifts, or educational purposes. Special editions may also be created to specification.
For details, contact Special Sales at 838 Lake Street S., Forest Lake MN 55025 or by email at sales@cartechbooks.com.

Title page:
Photo courtesy Pete Skiba.

DISTRIBUTION BY:

Europe
PGUK
63 Hatton Garden
London EC1N 8LE, England
Phone: 020 7061 1980 • Fax: 020 7242 3725
www.pguk.co.uk

Australia
Renniks Publications Ltd.
3/37-39 Green Street
Banksmeadow, NSW 2109, Australia
Phone: 2 9695 7055 • Fax: 2 9695 7355
www.renniks.com

Canada
Login Canada
300 Saulteaux Crescent
Winnipeg, MB, R3J 3T2 Canada
Phone: 800 665 1148 • Fax: 800 665 0103
www.lb.ca

CONTENTS

Dedication

This book is dedicated to those who can't leave well enough alone.

To the tinkerers.

To the dreamers.

To the *volks* who haunt swap meets and roam car shows.

To those who keep files stuffed full of ideas and shelves full of parts.

Most of all, it's dedicated to the next generation of air-cooled Volkswagen owners—in particular, those who find room in their hearts, garages, and bank accounts for the most iconic model of them all: the Type 1, the one and only Beetle.

May you find inspiration in these pages. Whatever you do to your Bug, we'd love to see it and hear your story.

Acknowledgments

As with our first CarTech book, *How to Restore Your Volkswagen Beetle*, this new primer on customizations and modifications took an entire village of VW experts to create.

People reach a point in middle-age when they become more acutely aware of time passing. As Airkooled Kustoms gets closer to its two-decade anniversary, the drive to keep the air-cooled Volkswagen hobby going is growing stronger too. Writing a book (or multiple books) is no easy task.

Having a writer "in the family" makes such a project possible, but in the ordinary course of business, we all tend to stay in our own lane: The body guys weld and grind. The paint guys wield paint guns and polishers. The mechanics wrench and eat jerky. The writer wrangles "squiggly" letters.

Producing this book, as with the last one, stretched us all. We wanted not only to introduce Beetle owners to the world of modification possibilities but also to some of the craftspeople, artists, and suppliers on which our shop relies to create highly personalized air-cooled VWs and Porsches. We are grateful for the generous input from these partners. They wrote notes, subjected themselves to rigorous interrogations (okay, friendly interviews), and took time away from doing what they love best to help us get this book into your hands.

We also want to give special thanks to Everett Barnes, founder of TheSamba.com, for allowing us to include excerpts from their extensive glossary compiled by thousands of Volkswagen lovers over the course of many years.

We are indebted to this book's expert contributors as well. They include John Alba of Grumpy's Metal, Jason Fields of Rare Air Mfg, Steve "Fish" Fisher of Doug's Buggs and Bunnies, Kerry Pinkerton of Imperial Wheeling Machines, Pete Skiba of Airkewld, and Don West of West Coast Wipers.

When someone drives or drags their prized vehicle to our shop, we fully understand the solemn trust that is placed in us. Car owners hand us their memories and dreams. We strive (in all things) to do it right. Many of our clients come from far away. We will likely never see their Beetles again after they leave the shop. However, we will always carry the satisfaction that comes from helping a Dub owner achieve the dream that they brought to us.

In an age where new cars come fully loaded with technological marvels that were unimaginable to early Volkswagen owners, it takes a certain kind of driver to appreciate the Beetle. Despite the popularity of the "new" Beetle, for the vintage crowd, there is no substitute for the original. While it's unlikely that a bone-stock-loving purist would ever crack the spine on this book, we want to give them a shout-out of appreciation. And for those of you who recognize the blank-canvas nature of your Beetle, we wish you the courage to try new things and the bank account to accommodate your wildest dreams.

Thank you, also, to CarTech. There are so many different makes and models in the automotive world, and you've published books to serve enthusiasts of every ilk. We appreciate your contribution to the Volkswagen-loving community and are proud to play a role in keeping the hobby alive.

Foreword

By Paul Cave
Founder of *VolksAmerica*
and *VolksMania* magazines

I know of no other classic car that intrigues and radicalizes a nation of crazy car drivers more than the VW Beetle. It is easy to get hung up on a variety of older automobiles to the extent that they drive you to distraction, but the charm of the Beetle is that it hangs around a lot longer than most others. What entices the Beetle lover is a machine that has a pretty face, demands of it the attention of a Tamagotchi, and gives back with the affection of a purring pet. Do tortoises purr?

With its inherent slow pace, determined grip, and ruggedness for on- and off-road conditions, which is all encapsulated within a contoured roofline that defies aerodynamic logic, the VW Tortoise certainly has appeal. Thank heavens that the name never caught on, and the VW Tamagotchi was never going to be a contender. But the VW Beetle, it's the stuff of legends!

The car's foibles have become its finest selling points and remain highly desirable. Such unconventional pieces were described as assets on the showroom floor, and we were well and truly in cahoots with air-cooling. So convinced were we after the fact that we reiterated the salesman's patter to the next Beetle buyer at resale. Hearty recommendations to a complete stranger or a quick shifty before counting the wad of cash in sweaty palms? It made no difference. Different is good, as we're told by a giant German food outlet that knows a good deal when it sells it.

Let's face facts: The car had unorthodox styling. It was noisy and often too hot or too cold on the inside. It was weirdly smelly. Its doors were difficult to close unless vented. It was never fast but rarely last. It offered a curious buffeting air around one's ears whenever the window was lowered to breathe, and you only got two wind-up windows. It was unlike any popular car seen before or after, and yet we fell for its craziness hook, line, and stinker.

The car's genius was its ability to take abuse and not to live out its worth as quickly as the rest. Those clever marketeers sold us the truth—albeit cleverly discussed as the truth. It was, was it not, the ugly car that got us there eventually and economically? And here we are today, when so many other car brands remain indistinguishable from their predecessors. You can always spot a Beetle, but you can't kill the Bug!

As a motoring journalist specializing in air-cooled Volkswagens, it's been my privilege to pull them apart in my own garage on two continents. They were built that way, after all, and easily capable of world travel through the toughest of terrains.

The body separates from the floor by releasing several bolts along each side and a few under the back seat. The floor has a central backbone running from the front to the back that acts in two very important ways: (1) to disguise a series of rods, pipes, and cables that are best left unseen and (2) to stiffen the body so that the doors might close properly. To this *chassis* is attached more bolted-on parts of equal importance, such as the front suspension and the rear transaxle.

The engine hangs off the back of the transaxle, and its removal is simplicity itself if you don't mind launching the car skyward. Sometimes you come across a Beetle with an engine that has never been removed. It's rare, but it does happen, and it doesn't always signify a miracle. The brakes are antiquated, the steering is light and vague, and the horn goes *beep beep*. It's no Road Runner, but it does have a habit of surviving no matter what rocks are thrown at it. It can take the cold of the arctic and heat of the desert or even float in the sea with a little persuasion. However, what's most appealing of all is that it transcends opinions and paychecks. It simply is the classic car for everyone, and it's intriguing what such a car can become in modern times.

Anyone who shares the same passion for these cars as I do is a friend of mine. I'm rewarded every day with the task of writing for and designing the VW magazines *VolksAmerica* and *VolksMania*, and I get to chat every day with businesses and individuals who share their passion for the Beetle or one of its many siblings.

One such person whom I talk to a lot these days is Eric LeClair, who fronts the business Airkooled Kustoms. What fascinates me about Eric is that he gets to do what most of us Beetle-loving drivers dream about doing every day: he gets to modify Beetles his way, and he doesn't have a TV! What? He calls the Airkooled Kustoms way of building stuff *the dark side*, and I know exactly what he means. It's epic cinema on wheels, which was born mostly in the early 1950s through late 1970s and reborn for the digital age.

It's no wonder that Eric describes himself as a kinetic artist as he fashions VW Beetles for the road with a certain look that's (if you'll excuse the pun) air-levitating. Airkooled Kustoms literally lifts the Beetle guise to another level.

Eric has amassed a level of knowledge about these cars and the wonderful things that can be done with them. He knows what works, what works better, and how to improve the cars before bolting them back together with a level of detail of which most could only dream. This ranges from fitting air-conditioning to enhanced braking and from slick transmissions to total body makeovers—everything inside and out.

It's the VW distraction in our own lives that keeps us going as Beetle enthusiasts. For Eric, it's the aesthetics of form and function at the customer level that floats his Bug. But the best bit is that he's prepared to share his knowledge through books, knowing that his suggestions and style of creativity will further enhance an appreciation for the little German classic.

The ability to turn a pile of rusty junk into a thing of beauty is not beyond the abilities of most classic car owners. It takes time, commitment, and special guidance to see the build through to a successful conclusion.

From car event to car event, magazine to magazine, the fluid-like approach to forming a design is for most an evolutionary process. Nothing feels better than achieving something yourself, and a nod of appreciation to those whose ideas were borrowed is often part of the story that unfolds in the likes of *VolksAmerica* and *VolksMania*. Suddenly, a car that was cloned millions of times and built to boogey from Point A to Point B has a stronger personality, and it wants to share it with you and others just like you.

Most of us may never build our own home, but we may well have a say in the interior design. Those tiles weren't actually made by you, were they? A car build is similar in so many ways. As a car builder or modifier, you'll excel in certain aspects but may fear to tread in other areas. The result will still be yours to drive and reconnect with.

You'll have a sense of achievement by sharing your passion with a car that's as individual as you. Some of the mysteries and fears of a rebuild can be tamed through text. This book aims to turn that anxiety into an understanding and appreciation of the difficult tasks ahead.

You cannot overlook what you don't know.

There are too many parts to a Volkswagen Beetle for any one person to know them all and understand how they interact with one another. For that, we have the specialists upon which to rely. For Eric's book about building and modifying the classic Beetle from the kinetic workshop of Airkooled Kustoms, he reached out to specialists to lend their knowledge to us all in one easy-to-read tech book. It gently summarizes what may work for you during your own rebuild and what may work just a little bit better. It opens your mind, permits you to move forward with confidence, and enables the creativity within us all.

With decades of knowledge in the industry, the book's author encourages and promotes you to follow the correct procedures and defines in detail how to create the classic VW Beetle of your dreams. Before long, you'll be muttering the words, "The next thing I'm going to do is . . ." and you'll know exactly where to turn (and probably which page too).

This book is built for a lifetime of fun in the classic VW Beetle garage.

Preface

To the uninitiated, that Beetle in your garage, under your carport, in your parking space, or even up on blocks is just a quirky old car. But to you (and to anyone else who caught a lifelong case of Dub Fever) it's much more.

Owning a Beetle is a lot like smoking a pipe in public. It's practically like issuing an invitation to passersby to share their stories: "Oh, my grandfather used to . . . ." "Wow, that brings back memories of when . . . ." "When I was a kid . . . ."

Beetles aren't the only cars still in circulation after multiple decades on the roads. Go to any car club show-and-shine, and you might see rides whose names faded into history half a century ago. It's not even uncommon to see some of the very first automobiles ever to leave an assembly line.

Of the 15 million Model Ts manufactured by Ford, it's reported that only about 500,000 are still in existence today. Enthusiasts restored them because they had memories of their parents or grandparents tinkering with them, they gravitated to the elegant simplicity of their inner workings, or because they're unusual, quirky, and cool.

It's a rarity to see them out on the roads, certainly during one's daily drive. That makes the odd appearance during a parade or other special event all the more intriguing. When we see one, we want to know what it's like to drive, how long it took to restore, how long the owner has had it, and more. It would be easy to stand around asking questions and dreaming of building our own.

As popular as the Model T and its descendants were and as long as its manufacturing run lasted, nothing compared to the Beetle. About 21 million rolled off the factory floor from 1938 to 2003. Multiple generations have seen Bugs on the roads (and in their own garages) as long as they've been alive. We have personal memories of our Volkswagens; it's not just an objective attraction.

When we see one that's been customized (radically or subtly) or restored, we must find out more. We want to know about that Beetle's lineage, how and where the owner found it, whether they did the modifications themselves, and more. While some Beetles are so old that their original owners are long gone, we still find the occasional original owner tooling around in their baby. More often, it's the second, third, or 10th owner's hands now caring for these old cars. Beetles only seem to grow closer to our hearts as the years and decades pass.

Indeed, a Beetle is transportation. However, it's also the automotive equivalent of a blank canvas. The iconic shape lends itself to customization. From stock to wildly customized, owners can make their Beetle *their* Beetle. While there will never be a shortage of opinions from onlookers about whether any particular modification should have been made, the fact remains that the vision for any ride belongs solely to the owner. While Beetles were built to be "the people's car," their owners are truly the only ones who have a legitimate say-so about how they look, sound, and feel to drive.

Perhaps you remember the 1965 children's book *Mr. Pine's Purple House*. Mr. Pine lived in a white house surrounded by a sea of other white houses that were indistinguishable. That is, until he started a customization project, so that his home would be distinctive. He planted a tree out front, and all of his neighbors did the same. He planted a bush. Same deal. Ultimately, he painted his white house purple and inspired his neighbors to branch out into every shade of the rainbow.

With a Beetle, the paint color is just the tip of the iceberg when it comes to customization. The range of preferences is exceptionally wide. There are the purists, who revel in their concours VW that is unmolested and pristinely preserved. However, once the door is opened to modifications, it's like a Pandora's box of endless options. Some are better than others, and some more or less generally appreciated. In the end, the possibilities are practically endless.

In many instances, form follows function for Beetle mods. Bigger engines, upgraded temperature control, modernized brakes, and increased creature comforts are modifications that you might not recognize unless you knew to look for them. In those cases, at the shop we say, "Stealth is style."

However, with other modifications, styling came first. Higher or lower stances, shiny bits added or shaved off, custom paint in every color imaginable, and even radical body modification are fair game when you want a custom ride. Some of these modifications became so popular that they earned a style name of their own, such as the California Look, the German Look, the Baja, or the Volksrod.

A funny thing happens when Beetle owners start tinkering with customization. A more recent children's book comes to mind: *If You Give a Mouse a Cookie*. As the slippery-slope story goes, if you give a mouse a cookie, it's going to want a glass of milk. It's going to want a straw, then a mirror (to check for a milk mustache), and on and on. As Beetle owners, we are that mouse. Once we start tinkering, we can't stop. We won't stop, in fact, until we have our cars exactly as we want them to be. Then, after some period of time, we get the itch to start modifying them further. We customize because we can.

It's common for Beetle owners to have a designated savings account for car parts. As with any long-term relationship, we invest time, money, and attention in our beloved. We gather with others who share an appreciation for Volkswagens. Some of us get tattoos depicting the object of our affection. We talk about them. We make plans. We dive deep to learn all we can.

Sometimes the drive to tweak, modify, and improve leaves us in a position of explaining the odd pile of parts in the garage or the mounting pile of purchases from our favorite VW parts houses. Beetle owners often get really good at persuading our partners to let us indulge our crazy obsession. They're good people, these family members who (even if they don't get it) get us.

As a vintage Volkswagen and Porsche restoration shop, Airkooled

Kustoms is proud to play even a small role in keeping the air-cooled passion alive. In a world where driverless cars are becoming inevitable, where entire generations are stumped when faced with a manual transmission, and a shrinking number of people know which end of a classic Beetle houses the engine, we still love the brutally elegant simplicity of a Dub. We could have chosen any make and model of vehicle to work with, but this is the specialty that chose us just as much as we chose it.

For most of us, Volkswagens are part of us. We bear the scars that come from decades of working on them. We still carry in our hearts the dream of "the one" that we must build someday.

We do what we can to promote the hobby, train the next generation, and build the Volkswagens that our clients remember or that they've long dreamed of owning. Mostly, we do full restorations. We take tired, rusty VWs back to piles of bare steel and then, in about a year, hand the client the keys to a brand-new, very old car. It's an expensive and time-consuming process. The parts are becoming harder and harder to find. So, that's part of the expense. But it's the labor that comprises the bulk of the price tag on these classics.

The level of care and concentration that goes into each build is like nothing you would ever see in an auto body or mechanical shop. Literally hundreds of hours go into perfecting the body so that the paint and polish look close to flawless. We're never actually happy with the vehicles we build; we only let the clients see them when we can stand the thought of doing so. Yet, we can't

get enough of this unique (if slightly maddening) opportunity to create kinetic art.

A restoration project is the perfect opportunity for owners to customize. Some want it stock. Others dare to face the wrath of purists and make radical changes to even the rarest of models. Throughout this book, you will see what we are doing to a four-month-only 1952 Zwitter.

To some, it will be glorious. To purists, it may be the cause for an aneurysm. A Zwitter is an extremely rare model that featured parts from two years combined in one Beetle. The Volkswagen factory was far too efficient and frugal to let perfectly good parts go to waste. So, in this model, you'll find the split back window of the earliest Bugs with the oval dash of the next model. Zwitter means *hermaphrodite* in German, which probably makes a lot more sense now.

This particular Zwitter spent decades under a tarp on the grounds of a junkyard in the Carolinas. The owner kept putting off a restoration for "someday" as many of us do. Year after year, a young man kept asking if he could buy it. However, the owner held onto his plan. It didn't matter to him that feral cats had taken up residence in the car, or that it was slowly succumbing to the ravages of rust.

The young man kept asking. Each time he went home to visit, he'd drive by the junkyard and have a chat with the owner, always parting by asking, "You ready to sell it yet?"

Finally, the owner said yes. That's when this Bug began its new life at nearly 70 years old. It's undergoing a complete restoration and will feature many of the modifications that are

discussed in this book.

You don't have to go the full restoration route to make your Beetle the way you want it, and you don't have to sell your organs on the black market to pay for a professional to make the modifications that you crave. Half of the battle is discovering your options and crafting a vision for your Beetle. The other part is the implementation.

Our hope is that this book will help you on both fronts. You'll discover a host of customizations that you can make to your Beetle and what's involved in making them. Whether you tackle the projects on your own or take your baby to a pro, you'll have a better idea of what to expect. The only limits on what can be done to customize your Bug come from your imagination and your wallet.

Whether you're a purist, a radical customization fanatic, or somewhere in between, we'd like to take this opportunity to thank you for your interest in our shared passion. The classic Volkswagen community is like no other, and it's an honor to be part of it with you. Nowhere else will you find such an enthusiastic, kind-hearted group of people who are hungry for knowledge and willing to share what they know. When you get the opportunity to talk with other Beetle nuts, make sure to learn something new. Together, we can keep this passion alive for future generations, but that's only if we pass along what we learn.

If you ever venture into north Alabama, reach out to Airkooled Kustoms in the city of Hazel Green. We'd love to show you around the shop, talk VWs, and meet your baby.

Take a Beetle chassis and modify it a bit, and you end up with the start of a Volkswagen Thing (left). Even the VW factory had modification on its mind. This two-wheel-drive, four-door convertible was produced from 1968 to 1983. They were only imported into the USA between 1973 and 1974.

When did the idea for the first Volkswagen Beetle modification dawn on anyone? It was likely about three seconds after the first Beetle rolled off the factory line. No doubt, it was before that imaginative scamp finished uttered, "Hey, what if we . . ." and one of the original purists scoffed and muttered, "If it ain't broke, don't fix it."

This 1968 Euro Beetle has lived its whole life being owned by the same family. Other than a disc brake upgrade for safety, it's about as stock as they come. Its name is Herbie, *of course. However, if you're looking for the famous numbers or racing stripes of its famous cousin, you're out of luck.*

The engineers behind this iconic car had three mandates to follow in its design: cheap to buy, simple to operate and maintain, and reliable enough to be safe on the Autobahn. Not only was that mission accomplished but they also created a vehicle that would become a crowd favorite. Between 1938 and 2003, 21,529,464 Beetles were sold around the world. It's a number that was highly publicized with the 2019 announcement that the Beetle's production days had come to a close.

Forget one in a million. For purists, it's enough for their ride to be one in 21 million. That's the goal, in fact, to keep their rides strictly stock. However, for those who can hardly look at a Bug without itching to lower it, make it faster, or modify some component or another, a bone-stock Beetle is merely a blank canvas waiting (practically begging) for modifications. They're in good company, those who've gone rogue.

In fact, the first people to modify

It could be said that the Super Beetle is a modification of the Beetle. While many VW enthusiasts consider "Fat Chicks" less desirable than Standard Beetles, everyone who sees Cherry Bomb agrees that it's pretty cool. The inspiration for this car began with its Porsche wheels and spread from there. (Photo Courtesy Bryan Bacon)

From the custom airbrushed artwork on the decklid to its 1,776-cc dual-port engine and 3-inch narrowed beam, this 1965 Beetle named Sandman is a good example of the retro California style. Sandman also sports a Wide 5 disc-brake upgrade and Freeway Flyer transmission as well as a Vintage Speed Classic shifter. (Photo Courtesy Bryan Bacon)

the Beetle were VW engineers themselves, demonstrating the perks that come with such a brutally simple design. In 1949, Volkswagen ordered the start of production on the Hebmüller, a coach-built conversion of the Beetle. The VW factory also used the same platform to build trucks that were used to cart components around the factory. The Karmann Ghia, the Thing, and ultimately, the prototype for the first Porsche took modification of the Beetle's chassis to a whole new level.

While few of today's hobbyists are likely to modify their Type 1s so extensively that they spawn a whole new vehicle model, in some cases, you might be hard-pressed to find much of the original design left. More commonly, owners customize their Beetles for better performance, handling, and appearance. Inside, outside, and even underneath, the clean slate of a stock Beetle lends itself to modification.

Customization and a Beetle's Value

It's a bit of a trick question. A vehicle's value lies in the eyes of the beholder or shopper.

For a purist looking at a customized ride, the mental math used to calculate its market value would involve the cost of returning it to stock. On the other hand, a modification fanatic looking at a stock Beetle would be tallying the cost of all the things they'll change.

There's a market for the virgin Beetle and the one that's been modified to within an inch of its life. The best advice is to do what makes you happy rather than looking for a financial return.

However, as the years stream by,

Modification options don't end when you open the door. You can make your Beetle more comfortable, safer, and even add modern amenities such as Bluetooth capability. Upgrades abound when it comes to seating options too, and you're not limited to Volkswagen seats. Many owners also upgrade their carpeting to make their Beetle unique.

pushing Beetles deeper into antique status, their marketplace value is climbing. Not every vehicle from decades in the past is worth restoring. As these Bugs become rarer and rarer, we see the effects of supply and demand. Once-less-desirable models are now sought after with an intensity that no one would have imagined 10 years ago.

One Beetle featured in this book serves as the perfect example of building and modifying to please only yourself. It's a 1952 Zwitter that is currently under restoration at Airkooled Kustoms. Our shop is located in Hazel Green, Alabama, and has been around since 2005—although nearly everyone involved in the shop has spent decades tinkering and wrenching on their own rides.

This coupe is extraordinarily rare. It was produced for only four months during a factory line change-over from November 1952 through early February 1953. It sports the dashboard of the oval model and the split-oval rear window of the original, and dealers offered the option of a tri-fold canvas ragtop. This one began life with a solid roof, though.

If a purist would see what we're doing to this very rare Beetle, he or she might have a coronary. Some of the customizations we'll show you feature a 1965 Karmann Ghia,

One of the first customization options to consider is the suspension height of your Beetle. This 1968 Euro Beetle is set at the stock height. While it won't win any limbo contests at a car show, there are many Beetles set so low that they scrape the pavement when driven.

which is obviously not a Beetle, but the available options and the process that you'll follow are the same. For those who've never seen a Beetle component that they didn't want to somehow tweak, this is the project of a lifetime; we are supremely honored that our client entrusted this project to our care. It will draw stares and drop jaws among customization fans, and it will likely incite insults and hate mail from purists.

While this Zwitter will be extremely customized, it's only fair to mention that we've taken a preservation measure that will provide some relief for purists. Rather than modifying its matching-numbers chassis, we've saved it unmolested in case the owner decides to sell someday. This ride is being built on a brand-new chassis that is reinforced to handle a much larger engine and all the components needed to support it.

The range of modifications that you could make is virtually endless. The price range for adding those custom elements is wide too. You'll find that when you start exploring your options, some require a simple swapping of parts. Others are far more complicated to achieve or to reverse.

Tip of the Iceberg

The list of possible customizations that you could make to your Beetle is virtually endless. A short list of common modifications includes:

- Baja
- Race cars
- Rat Rods
- Hot Rods (also called Volksrods)
- Chopped
- Slammed

Even among stock Beetles, it's wise to consider an upgrade from drum brakes to disc brakes. They have better stopping power, are self-adjusting, and are much easier to inspect during routine maintenance. You don't have to remove your wheels to take a look, and you'll find it easy to buy disc brake pads at your local auto parts store.

- California Style
- Australian Style
- Meyers Manx
- Trikes
- Electric vehicle conversions

In addition to making sweeping stylistic changes, nearly every component of a Beetle presents an opportunity for customization. We couldn't possibly list them all, much less cover them (at least not in a single book). What you will find here is information, guidance, and step-by-step directions for making the most popular modifications we see and do at our shop.

At Airkooled Kustoms, we couldn't do what we do (to the level that we do it) alone. That's why we rely on some of the most innovative and highly skilled specialists in the Volkswagen world. We draw on their expertise to create jaw-dropping rides for our clients. Likewise, we've tapped them to share their specialized knowhow with you here so that you can learn from the best in the world.

Maximum Value

If you're interested in simply changing superficial elements of your Bug, such as mirrors and car mats, you don't need this book. Just buy what you love and go with it. There are plenty of bolt-on parts that require the simplest of tools and practically no skills to install. Any changes you make will be easy enough to undo if you change your mind.

However, if you're considering more extensive modifications, this book will serve you well. Read it all the way through before you touch a wrench or buy a new part. As simple as the Beetle's design is, it's still a cohesive unit. If you change one part, it'll impact this, that, and the other part. It's like tipping the first tile in a line of dominoes.

That's particularly true if you want to modify the drivetrain. For example, a bigger engine requires a stronger suspension, a more robust transmission, and better brakes. By reading this book before you roll up your sleeves, you'll avoid inadvertently modifying your Beetle into a state of being undriveable.

Plus, you may find a modification option that you never previously considered. We tapped some of our favorite vendors—the companies that we trust to provide top-notch components and parts for the restorations that we do. You'll see what's hot on the modifications market and find out how to add them to your car.

There is no substitute for a good plan. This book will help you formulate a plan that includes all the modifications that you want to make in an order that makes sense. After all, as enjoyable as tinkering is, it's a lot more fun when you don't have to do rework because you didn't anticipate

This 1965 Beetle is an updated replica of the car that our clients took on their honeymoon when it was new. It features a 1,600-cc dual-port engine, Wide 5 disc brakes, a TMI interior, EMPI five-spoke chrome wheels, 2.5-inch drop spindles, and a 3-inch narrowed beam.

the impact that one customization had on the project as a whole.

As you read, keep a project notebook handy. Jot down your ideas, make lists, work out a budget, and plan your project on paper before you touch your car. This way, you can tackle your customizations in a way that makes sense for your schedule, budget, and preferences.

Here's a little cheerleading before we get started: You can do this! It's your Beetle, so whatever you deem fit to do is perfectly acceptable. Don't build it for anyone but you. You owe no one an explanation for your design choices. Also, even though some parts are becoming more scarce, there's been an upsurge in aftermarket parts suppliers and inventors.

In the end, there's nothing that you can do to your Beetle that can't be undone. (Okay, we didn't say that undoing it would be easy—just possible.) Be fearless.

BEFORE WE GET ROLLING

What's the one thing that you absolutely must have before you can modify your Beetle? Your Beetle, of course.

More than that, your Beetle must be sound enough to withstand modifications. After all, there's no point customizing a vehicle that you can never safely drive—unless you just want an interesting piece of wall art.

So, we're going to provide a quick guide you can use to buy a good project car. *Good* is a relative term, though. The proverbial cream puff of a car—one that never spent a night under the stars (or in a hail storm), never was rained on (or in), and never endured a chance encounter with a curb, a pole, or another vehicle—is a myth. Certainly, there may be one hidden somewhere. However, the truth is that the Beetle you'll be working on has probably been worked over by nature, the harsh realities of the driving world, and, most damaging of all, the ravages of time.

Here is a saying that is especially common among patina lovers: "Rust is not a crime." While it may not be a crime, it is a murderer. Rust is an unstoppable force, a cancer (seen or unseen) that eats your Beetle bite by bite. Wouldn't it be a shame to invest your time and money into making modifications that simply fall off when you drive and take along with them the components to which they were attached? Assess your Beetle's rust situation and remedy anything that is life-threatening before going any further.

It took the new owner of this rare 1952 Zwitter Beetle 26 years of persistence to finally persuade its former owner to agree to sell it. The modifications planned for this car will shock and stun purists and leave the custom crowd cheering. When it's your Beetle, you get to decide what happens to it.

Buy Once, Cry Once

That's a sentiment worth remembering throughout your project, which starts with buying your Beetle. Prices are rising steadily for Bugs, especially for those in good condition. You get what you pay for, so before plunking down your hard-earned cash on a *bargain*, consider the real cost. It's not uncommon for uninitiated buyers to bite off more than they can chew when it comes to bringing a car up to the level of being a running and driving vehicle.

If you have a Beetle already, great! That's probably the best one for you to modify. However, if you're in the market for one that you can make your own, you'll save time and money in the long run by buying one that's as close as possible to what you have in mind. For example, if you want a Baja Beetle, buy one rather than trying to convert one. There are still plenty of modifications you can make; there is no need to make it harder than necessary.

Bring some simple tools when you check out a prospective project car, including:

• Use a screwdriver or an awl to poke at any rusty areas. If the tool goes through, there's a lot of welding and metalwork in your future.

• Use a magnet to detect filler abuse—nearly every car this age has suffered dents and dings. Those are fine, but if you want to avoid needless heartache, avoid buying one with so much filler it's like the body shop frosted it like a cake. A small magnet won't stick to a body panel that's full of filler.

• Use a flashlight and hand mirror to check out the underside of the car if it is not on a lift.

• A crescent wrench and socket set may be useful as you examine the engine bay.

• A gas can, jumper cables, starting fluid, and even a spare battery will come in handy if you discover that the Beetle that "ran when I parked it" suddenly won't run.

Check for Rust

Unlike many modern cars, the Beetle body is made of steel. It's strong, of course, but it's much weaker if it's riddled with rust. Even with drain holes and rudimentary rustproofing, you'll see that the progression of corrosion is relentless.

The most vulnerable spots are the floor pan, battery tray (passenger-side rear), underneath the spare tire, the fender mounting points, the frame head, kick panels, door posts, rear parcel shelf, heater channels, firewall, strut towers (if you're getting a Super Beetle), and the bottom 4 to 9 inches of the body. If that sounds like a lot of vulnerable spots, you're right.

Check these areas carefully, looking for signs of repairs, rust mediation, and bubbling paint. It's not uncommon to find cars for which the cost of restoration greatly outstrips the purchase price. If you'd rather not begin your project so far behind the curve, start with a solid core. Some rust is virtually inescapable. These cars can be more than a half-century old. Rust happens.

We'll go into some detail about repairing rusty bits, but if you start with a car that's in good shape because those repairs have already been done well, you can skim through that discussion.

Check the Engine

Sure, Beetle engines are beautiful in their simplicity. However, don't make the mistake of thinking they're cheap. Removing your engine isn't exactly a cakewalk, either. If you decide to get a Bug with a bum engine or needs extensive restoration before you feel comfortable driving it, get

While rust can be beautiful on a patina ride, that corrosion will eat and eventually destroy your Beetle. Even if you decide to leave the patina intact, be sure to address the rust. Before modifying your car, it's important to make sure it's structurally sound. Do a thorough inspection to find the rust spots first.

If you need to source a Beetle for your modification project, check the engine before you buy. Even if you plan to upgrade to a faster engine, figure out what you're starting with. If it will run, that's a good sign. If it won't, it will be harder to check the other mechanical components.

Stopping and Going Are Equally Important

One of the first modifications that many Beetle owners make is upgrading the brake system from the standard drum brakes to disc brakes. It's a safety issue to address early on in your project.

Many owners make this swap without even considering keeping the original drum brakes. That's what we recommend, but if you're determined to stick with your Beetle's drum brakes, be sure that they work well.

Check the emergency brake, and watch how far the brake pedal sinks when you stop and how smoothly you stop. Also, examine the rubber hoses and brake lines for rust and rot. If the setup works, great. However, if you find problems or just want to make your Beetle as safe as possible, put a brake system switch at the top of your to-do list.

our first book, *How to Restore Your Volkswagen Beetle,* or *How to Rebuild VW Air-Cooled Engines: 1961–2003,* which are available at cartechbooks.com.

We're only halfway joking when we say we've never met a Beetle that didn't have an oil leak. It's a very common problem that shows up most frequently as a valve cover, sump plate, pushrod tube, or case half leak. The flat 4-cylinder configuration poses a challenge if water has entered the engine and rusted the piston rings and valves.

Begin with a visual inspection to make sure that all of the engine components are there. Then, start it up. If it doesn't start right up, remove the spark plugs and give the cylinders a squirt of penetrating oil. You may need to use a wrench to turn the engine by the crank pulley. Watch for smoke and listen

for weird noises such as knocking or pinging.

Conduct a test drive and pay attention to the gauges. If the oil light comes on, don't ignore this warning sign. Oil pressure problems mean that the engine's not getting enough oil to run smoothly or live long. Also, watch for crankshaft issues. The Beetle's engine is perfect for high mileage at low RPM, but a lifetime of quick acceleration can lead to a bent crankshaft, which can damage the case, break the rods, and send your flywheel flying. It's all fixable, of course, but it's best if you know what work is in store ahead of time.

If you're planning to replace the engine, the current powerplant's condition won't matter as much. Still, you can deduce a lot about the car's overall upkeep by examining the engine. Knowledge is power!

It's smart to upgrade from drum brakes to disc brakes if stopping is important to you. You can paint or powder coat your disc brakes to make them match your Beetle. This set has yet to be customized, but ultimately, it will be painted to coordinate with the body.

This is a swing axle. You can see how the new disc brakes connect to the transmission. We've painted it with an industrial-strength enamel that will increase its durability and help stave off rust.

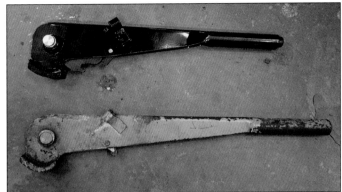

As you inspect a prospective project car to modify, pay attention to the emergency brake. Pull it up and see how it performs. Replacing a worn-out emergency brake isn't very complicated, but you should know its condition so that you can plan ahead.

If you're planning to install a bigger engine, you may not care much about the transmission you have right now. It'll need upgrading along with other components that we'll discuss in chapter 5. However, if you keep the original engine or replace it with an equivalent, your existing transmission may work just fine.

Transmissions are pricey, so it's important to know what you have and how well it will work. You can tell a lot during a test drive if you shift through all of the gears. Be on the alert for grinding between gears, an overly stiff or loose clutch, and instances of popping out of gear. These are sure signs of issues you'll need to address.

Check the Suspension

At the shop, our tastes run toward the dramatically lowered suspension. If it's scraping the ground, it's probably low enough! This is a very common modification to make, and we'll cover some options in upcoming chapters for the low- or high-minded among you. However, if you like your Beetle at standard height, pay attention to the suspension. Beetles built through 1965 have a king

Here's an installed 4-inch narrowed adjustable beam. By narrowing your front beam, you can go low with your suspension. The reason for narrowing the beam is to tuck your rims into the body so that they don't hit the fenders when turning. You can also fit larger rims and tires within the wheel well.

This low-riding Beetle is a great example of a patina ride with attitude. While you might need to slow way down to clear speed bumps, you will look good doing so. Many low-slung Bug fans find the standard-height suspension to be too high after they get used to the low look.

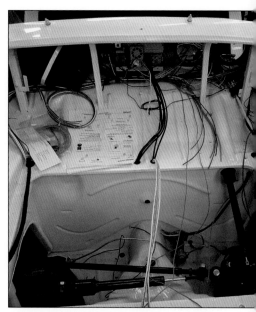

See the notches on the torsion arm? They are there to prevent interference with the suspension stops on a lowered vehicle. Without them, every time you go over a bump, the bar will hit the pan's upper shock mount guides.

Check the wiring on the Bug you plan to restore. Unless the car has already undergone restoration, it's likely that the wiring is overdue for an upgrade. Look for worn, cracked, and burnt areas as a clear indication that it's time for a new wiring harness.

Over the years, most Beetles' wiring systems wind up hacked and dodgy because not everyone enjoys following the wiring diagram. The wires won't last forever, as the insulation can eventually degrade to the point where you experience electrical shorts. While replacing the harness isn't exactly a modification, it's a good idea to do if you haven't already.

and link pin setup in the front end. After that, the factory switched to ball-joint front beams.

As you test drive the Beetle, pay attention to how the car handles. It's very helpful to have a friend drive separately behind you to watch too. If the steering feels loose, the car handles poorly, one side rides higher than the other (often, the driver's side is lower than the passenger's side after decades of driver-only driving), or the Beetle looks like it's moving on a diagonal plane, you have a suspension issue.

Inspect the Wiring

As decades pass, wires wear out and can become unreliable or even unsafe. Replacing the wiring harness is a wonderful idea if it's feasible, but it's not exactly a simple process. If any modifications are planned that will involve removing the body from the pan, seriously consider upgrading and replacing the wiring harness at that time because it'll be easier.

Either way, inspect your Beetle's wiring. You might be surprised to see how *creative* some VW owners

get with their wiring. Pop the front hood to examine the wiring behind the dashboard as an indicator of possible issues. Also, look at the wiring running along the front wheel wells.

Coming from the factory, the wires were encased in metal or rubber tubing (depending on the year). If anyone has hacked the wiring, you'll be able to see that immediately because the tubing will be gone. Also look for brittleness, discoloration, burns, and wear; these are sure signs that the years have been unkind to the wiring. It would be a shame to get your Beetle customized to your liking only to have it catch on fire from an electrical problem. So, please give serious consideration to making this upgrade.

After your car comes back from blasting, you'll have no problem spotting the rusty bits that need replacing. In some cases, sandblasting takes off a substantial portion of the car body, including the lower 6 to 9 inches. While it can be disheartening to discover the damage oxidation has done, it's better to know so you can fix it before going further.

You can either take your vehicle to a sandblasting business or find one that will come to your location. It's noisy, sandy, and takes several hours to do a thorough job. This is the best way to get a thorough assessment of the extent of corrosion in your vehicle.

Now, About that Rust

In a perfect world, the Beetle that you want to modify would magically roll into your driveway already rust-free and solid so that you can get to the fun part faster. This is not that world. You're probably looking at doing some rust remediation before you go any further. After all, there's no point in spending good money on upgrades that'll fall off of your rust bucket as you drive.

When performing a full restoration, strip your Beetle back to bare metal first. In its naked state, you'll be able to see the body's condition clearly. Then, repair or replace any panels and parts that have a corrosion problem before going any further.

Since we're not detailing what goes into a full-scale restoration in this book, you'll need to gauge how sound the Beetle's body is and tackle whatever bodywork makes sense. Pay particularly close attention to the

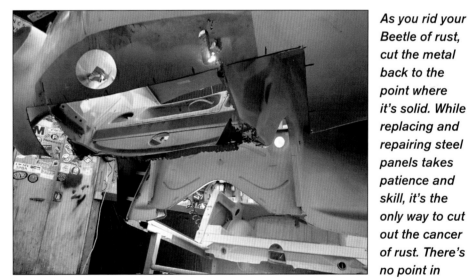

As you rid your Beetle of rust, cut the metal back to the point where it's solid. While replacing and repairing steel panels takes patience and skill, it's the only way to cut out the cancer of rust. There's no point in adding custom touches to your car if they're in danger of falling off as you drive because of rust.

bottom of the heater channels, the area by the wheel wells on the inner fender wells, and the floor pans and the battery tray (if any overcharging led to an acid leak) as you perform a thorough inspection. Remember that there's always 30 to 50 percent more rust lurking beneath the surface than what you can see.

With that said, determine whether your ride needs to go into rough metal or finish metal for rust abatement. With rough metal, you'll replace and repair metal that's been dented, dinged, or corroded. If the damage on your car is limited to small flaws in the steel, you can get by only using finish metal techniques. Of course,

Buy the highest-quality hammers and dollies that you can afford. These are on the pricey end of the spectrum: Martin's. Another brand we recommend is Eastwood. With lower-quality hammers and dollies, you'll find that the flat hammers aren't all that flat and the picks aren't very sharp.

This is a Lincoln 140 welder with variable voltage and speed. It's a very good entry-level welder and is available online as well as from local welding companies. If you buy a good one, you can get 15 to 20 years of service from it.

TECH TIP — Rough Metal

Gather the following tools and equipment:
• Grinder
• Cutoff wheel
• Sanding disc
• Welder
• Protective clothing for welding (leather gloves, leather jacket, and welding helmet)
• Hammer and dolly
• Sheet-metal screws

whether you do the work yourself or send your Beetle out for body repairs depends on your skills, budget, and whether you want to invest the time learning some new skills.

Can You Weld?

If you're not an experienced welder, get a copy of CarTech's *Weld Like a Pro*. After you get the gist of the process, the next step is trying it on your own. Get some scrap metal that's clean and free of paint, oil, and dirt so that you can practice. You may be able to borrow a welder from a fellow classic car enthusiast. If not, get one of your own. You will get exactly what you pay for, so invest in the best welder that you can afford.

Welding Safety

If you value your eyesight and skin, take welding safety seriously. Get a quality helmet with auto-darkening technology. It will be similar to wearing very dark sunglasses, until the arc strikes. Then, it automatically protects your eyes while allowing you to look directly at the weld safely. Don't settle for a cheap helmet; you might think you're protected, but it's likely that you'll get the equivalent of a sunburn and might even suffer damage to your vision.

Panel Replacement

If you have body panels that are rusty beyond repair, replace them. You'll also need to treat the body

You can trace out a replacement panel to rebuild a section that has been eaten by rust. Make sure to draw your cut lines on the near side of where you intend to cut so you don't go overboard and take too much steel off.

Ideally, you'll leave a 1/16-inch gap. These clamps will ensure an even gap all the way around. That way, you'll have the correct spacing for welding. They're fairly inexpensive and available online. Welds can only effectively fill a space of 1/16 inch and maintain their integrity, so using clamps can make the job a lot easier.

Here's an example of dot welding. The original panels are 19 gauge. Good replacement panels are also 19 gauge; although, you will likely find other thicknesses. Dot welding will keep heat distortion to a minimum. You'll add a dot weld every couple of inches, allow the metal to cool, and then go back to fill in the missing dots.

After you weld, it's time to grind. Remove excess welding material without getting into the parent steel. Just take enough of the weld off to make it level with both panels on either side of the weld. Keep your heat down to avoid distorting the panels.

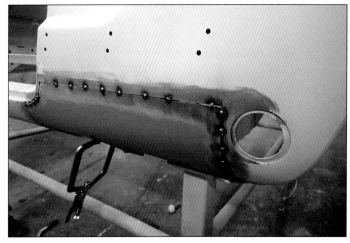

Here's an example of tack welding. The goal is to get the panel in place with a first pass. As you weld, remove the clamps; the weld will hold the panel in place. Make sure you leave 1 to 3 inches between welds to minimize heat distortion in the surrounding metal. If you know how to sew, think of tack welds as basting stitches.

with chemical rust treatment to prevent corrosion from immediately setting back in. You may be surprised to find that brand-new panels from aftermarket suppliers fit imperfectly without some adjustment.

Use your replacement panel as a guide. Trace your cutting lines about 1/16 inch inside where you need to cut, so you don't take off too much material. Make sure that your cut line leaves you with solid metal. You don't want to join new panels to rusty areas. Use a grease pencil or permanent marker. As you fit the panel, gradually remove material to create a 1/16-inch gap between the panels. That gap will allow the weld to penetrate well.

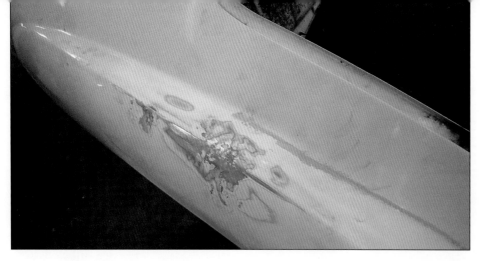

Parking lot dings happen when shopping carts escape their corral. Fifteen minutes with a hammer and dolly can do wonders for pulling the dents out. Choose a hammer and dolly that closely matches the size and shape of the area where you're working.

Use zip screws to hold the panel in place while you work. Then, remove them as you go, welding the holes closed. Avoid warping the panels by keeping your heat to a minimum and not lingering on any area for too long. Just weld with short *dots* and then sand or grind the area down afterward. Be sure that your welder's settings match the gauge of the metal that you're welding. Welders are not all the same; check the inside flap to get the proper heat and wire speed settings for your machine.

If you need to replace any panels, buy the best quality you can afford. There's a significant difference in the thickness as well as the composition of the steel. Save yourself some work by getting panels already stamped into the shape you need when you buy from a metal fabricator. New old stock (NOS) parts are left over from the original production stock and are a good option if you can find them.

After you finish welding, grind the welds down flat to match the original panel's thickness. Don't linger too long in any spot with the grinder. If you do, you can overheat the metal and cause warping.

Once you're happy with the panel, treat it with metal etch and then use phosphoric acid to prepare it for filler. Do this to make sure that you've addressed any oxidation you can't see. Wipe down every panel with phosphoric acid, including the panels' undersides and inside any crevices and cavities. Preventing rust is worth the extra effort.

If you want your Beetle to look smooth and straight, the work's not done until you've completed some hammer and dolly work in what is called the finish metal stage. Metal

TECH TIP

Finish Metal Tools

On the right, we have the result after beating the dents out with a hammer and a dolly. On the left, you can see what happens after taking the next step of using the shrinking disk. Getting your car smooth and straight takes time, elbow grease, good tools, and a lot of patience.

Gather the following tools and equipment:
- Selection of body hammers
- Basic set of body dollies to match the size and shape of the panel
- Slapping spoons
- Shrinking disc
- Latex gloves
- Air nozzle for the compressed-air line

- Fillers: Kevlar-infused epoxy (Kitty Hair) and Evercoat's Extreme Gold
- Dual-action sander (DA) and an assortment of grits: 40, 80, 120, 220, 320/400, 600
- Primer and gun
- Red Scotch-Brite pads
- All the patience that you can muster

TECH TIP

Feel for Flaws

Don't rely only on your eyes to make sure your panels are straight. Run your hands and fingertips over each panel to search for invisible flaws. If you're working on small areas, a jeweler's torch is helpful for heating the metal. This is an advanced technique, and you'll need to be sure to cool the metal.

holds a memory of the way it was originally pressed. Dings and dents can be coaxed back into their pre-collision state with some persuasion.

By spending the time and elbow grease required to smooth it all out, the amount of filler needed in the next step can be minimized. Steel is always preferable to filler, so this is worth the effort. At our shop, the goal is no more than 1/32- to 1/16-inch filler thickness. The industry standard allows for as much as 1/8 inch of filler. If you want to really do it

right (and to understand what you're doing), pick up CarTech's book *Automotive Sheet Metal Forming and Fabrication*, which is an in-depth guide.

Finish Metalwork

This phase of bodywork involves using a shrinking disc to heat the top layer of steel using friction. Then, cool it off with water to help smooth it out. Select the smallest and most recent dings and dents to work with first.

Start by placing an appropriately sized dolly in the center point of the dent or ding. Holding it in place with one hand, use a finishing hammer in the other hand. Starting at the outside point of the dent, work in a circular pattern, moving inward toward the center. Don't move the dolly. When you've reached the center of the dent, use a slapping spoon to go back over your work area, dispersing the force of the hammer. If you stretch the metal too far, just use some cool water with your shrinking disc to get the steel back into shape.

Filler

While we're not huge fans of filler, it's possible to use just a little bit to smooth out any panels that still need some help. Only work with a good two-stage filler (skip the single-stage varieties) and some fine sandpaper for blending.

Three types of filler are available:

Epoxy Resin

Epoxy resin is durable, even in places where heat, high vibration, and excessive wear can take a toll. Use just a little bit on doorjambs and the engine bay.

Talc-Based Filler

Talc-based filler is the best type used for minor surfacing.

Spot Filler

Use this lightweight material to fill pinholes and minor scratches.

Skip the plastic spatulas and get a set of metal spreading spatulas instead. This will help you hold a working edge so that you get a smooth result. Likewise, don't go cheap and disposable on the mixing board. Get a glass one so that you can clean, scrape, and reuse it. Never use a cardboard mixing board because the oil and wax in the cardboard will leach into the panel surface and cause adhesion problems when you paint.

When you mix the filler, be sure to follow the manufacturer's instructions. Don't over- or under-catalyze,

This is everything you need to work with filler. It's best to get your tools and equipment together so you can grab what you need when you need it. Select an assortment of tools and supplies of varying sizes and grits so that you can use the correct tool for the job.

Your paint job is only as good as the underlying materials. Choose a good, high-quality paint line and stick with it from the sealer all the way through the clear coat. The chemistry is made to be compatible throughout the process so that you can minimize adhesion issues. Get the highest-quality paint gun you can afford. We have a designated gun for sealer, another for high build, another for color, and a final gun for clear.

and don't skimp on the hardener. Mix using a downward motion rather than whipping it or stirring. The goal is to avoid adding air into the mix. This way, you'll avoid pinholes and voids in the surface. You'll notice that the filler's color shifts slightly when you mix. Keep mixing until the color is uniform.

Apply the filler by using two metal spatulas. Choose one that's a bit bigger than the area you're working on and one that's about the same size as the area. Only apply a very thin layer of filler at a time. You can always add more, but if you use too much from the start, adhesion problems will surface when you paint. When you complete each pass with the spatula, knock off any excess material from the edges.

After letting the filler cure (following manufacturer's specifications),

take a hand block or pneumatic tool to knock any high spots down. With rough filler, choose sandpaper with 80 to 120 grit. For finer filler, go with 180 to 220 grit. If you're using glaze putty, start with 320 grit and finish with 400. Once the filler phase is complete, apply sealer and then paint as you wish.

Safety

A quick word about shop safety is in order. Depending on the customizations that have been chosen for your car, you may be working with flammable, heavy, electrical, or noxious materials. You'll be using sharp, fast-moving tools with the potential to crush, scrape, or burn. Understand and follow the safety precautions for all tools, components, and materials. Don't try to lift more than is safe.

Work in a well-ventilated and well-lit space.

It's also important to keep a clean work area, which will help you avoid tripping over tools and parts and potentially injuring yourself or damaging your car. Plus, you'll minimize dirt and other contaminants settling on your project. Finally, you'll be glad that you can find the tool or part that is needed when you need it. It's a lot more enjoyable to make progress on your car than it is to waste time hunting for what you need.

Now that you have a sound, strong car body with which to work, it's time for the really fun stuff: starting your modifications. Because you spent this time preparing your Beetle, the customization touches you'll add next will *hold* rather than *fall off* in a shower of rust dust.

CUSTOM WHEELS

Any fashionista will say that shoes make the outfit, and it's no different with cars, really. That's why one of the most commonly customized bits of a Beetle is the wheels. However, there's more to wheels than meets the eye.

With footwear, a poor choice can look awful, be uncomfortable, and even prove to be downright dangerous in extreme cases. But with your Beetle's wheels, it's the same deal. Of course, when it comes to looks, beauty is in the eye of the beholder. So, we won't share our strong

Porsche Turbo Twist 7- and 9-inch wheels will fit your Dub with the correct set of spacers. The rears need a 9-mm spacer, and the fronts (7 inches) need a 3-mm spacer and a longer set of studs.

Powder coating your rims and installing a new set of hubcaps are simple bits of customization that you can do. While it might not be blingy, it is period correct.

Sometimes wider fenders are needed to make your rims look right on your ride: 4 inches in the rear and 2 inches on the front. Make note of where your wheel sits on the body. (Photo Courtesy Bryan Bacon)

A custom-made rim is not out of reach. The 4-inch rims on a Wide-5 bolt pattern (5/205) rim on a narrowed beam will tuck in well and look sharp.

opinions about wheels much here, as it's purely subjective. Some owners like the look of wheels so small that it's reminiscent of a little kid playing dress-up in a parent's clothes. Others like a "meaty" look with extra rubber. Still others like the look of a little car on huge wheels.

That's all a matter of personal preference, and it's up to you to decide what you like. However, we need to have some discussion about compatibility, fit, and finish. A wheel is only "just a wheel" to someone who doesn't know what they're looking at, after all.

Theoretically, any wheel could be made to fit a Beetle. If you doubt that fact, search online for a Beetle monster truck. We'll reserve comment, other than to say that yes, technically, any wheel can be made to fit any vehicle. It's your Beetle, of course, and you should do what pleases you.

Simple Swaps and Styles

Assuming that you want to preserve the silhouette of your Bug, at least for the most part, look at wheels that are compatible for your ride. You can get a custom look without having to do major reconstructive surgery on your car. The simplest option is to replace your existing wheels with an equivalent model.

Many online wheel distributors and manufacturers can help you identify great options. Just tell them what kind of wheels you have, including the bolt pattern. Then, they'll help you find an easy swap

A good, cost-effective choice is a set of aftermarket rims. The EMPI eight-spoke wheel is a true classic that will bolt right up.

you could make over the weekend. You will find various finishes from chrome to steel, and if you're painting your VW, you might want to paint your wheels while you're at it.

You can customize the look of your wheels without actually changing them. There are trim rings, hubcaps, center caps, tire styles, and many more options available from most Volkswagen parts houses. Just be sure to ask the customer service

Painted wheels and a wide beauty ring were available as a dealer option. They are now being reproduced in high-quality chrome. With the factory baby moon hubcaps and a thin white-wall, they will make an understated statement.

There are a few rim manufacturers. This is a well-done copy of a BRM wheel. It has been remanufactured and made available for Volkswagens.

This is a classic look on a classic ride. Wide whitewall tires are an expensive upgrade, but they are well worth every penny. These come from Coker Tire out of Chattanooga, Tennessee.

department before you buy to verify that the accessories you love will actually fit with your wheels.

Not-so-Simple Options

Now, if you want to get a bit more creative, there will be math involved—also some physics if we're going to be completely up front with you. You also need to understand bolt patterns and how all of this impacts your comfort and safety on the road.

The wheels you roll will impact how your Beetle performs, how safely and comfortably you ride, your fuel economy, and how noisy your ride is. Even a seemingly innocent decision, such as the height of your tires' side-walls, can make a dramatic change to your driving experience.

The shorter the sidewall, the better the handling in general. The road noise, vibration, and harshness (NVH) are typically better with smaller wheels. Of course, how it all works on your specific Beetle depends on any modifications that you've made to the suspension height and whether you've narrowed your beam.

With no fenders, the sky is the limit. These rims are destined for a custom-built trike. You don't have to pay much attention to the offset to run these.

While these rims/wheels look stock, they are not. This is a reproduction of an OEM rim that is offered in 4.5- and 5.5-inch rim widths.

Bolt Patterns

Until 1967, Beetles had what's called a "Wide-5" bolt pattern: 5/205 mm, for example. That's easy enough to identify, assuming that you can count to five! From 1968 onward, when the Volkswagen factory switched Beetle manufacturing to feature disc brakes, it switched the wheels from five bolts to four.

Most five-bolt wheels are interchangeable with each other. It's the same with the four-bolt version, 4/130 mm, for example. However, you're not limited to sticking with what you have. There are ways to use spacers and adapters to make other wheel types work with your Bug. Porsche wheels are a popular choice.

You'll need to know how to understand bolt pattern numbers or classifications. There are two numbers involved. The first number is the number of bolt holes in the wheel. The second number gives a key measurement from one hole to another, depending on how many bolts that wheel has.

On an even-numbered bolt pattern, measure from the center of one hole to the center of the hole next to it. For an odd-numbered bolt pattern, it's a bit different: measure from the center of one hole to the center of the hole two holes away.

There are bolt pattern gauges available if you want to get more technical. There are also very complicated geometric equations that you can delve into if you like that kind of thing.

Width, Offset, and Backspacing

Getting the ride you want with the wheels you love is going to involve some measuring and

This is the 5 x 205 bolt pattern on a 5.5-inch rim. It's mostly available on pre-1966 Bugs. It's a classic look that's easy to bolt on and go.

Nothing beats a classic, period-correct aftermarket rim with a stamp date of 1969. An EMPI eight-spoke rim with a set of knockoffs finishes the look.

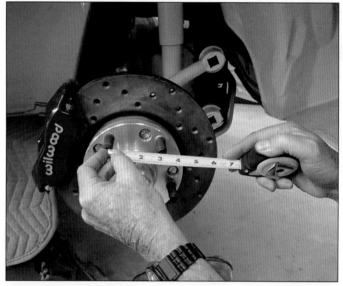

With an odd number of studs, skip a stud while measuring. Center to center is the most accurate way to take this measurement.

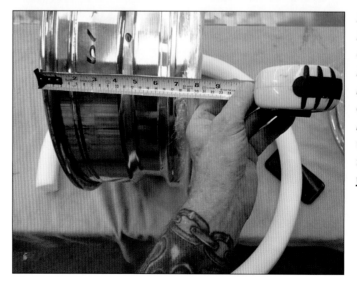

Measuring the rim bead width, go center to center. Note that different manufacturers have different sidewall measurements, which can change the clearance of your fenders.

When measuring your rim, take the inside-to-inside measurement. You'll get the most accurate set of numbers for determining your tire size.

The centerline measurement requires two measurements. Go from the inside mounting face to the back of the rim. Then, go from the inside mounting face to the front side of the rim.

Offset and backspacing are also measured from the inside of the mounting face. This will determine how close the rim gets to the inner fender well of the car.

Test fit the rims on your car with your brakes installed before you order tires. This will spare you some headaches as you figure out your tire size.

math. It is better to suffer through these calculations before setting your heart on wheels that won't work without significant body modifications.

Determine your wheel width, which is bead lip to bead lip. As simple as it sounds, it's easy to measure incorrectly. To measure your wheel width correctly, measure from the bead lip on one side to the bead lip on the other side. This measurement will be different from the actual wheel width, so it can be a little confusing.

The offset is the next measurement you'll make, and it's the distance from the mounting surface to the center of the wheel. If you were to draw a line down the middle of the wheel, the offset would be the distance from the back of the mounting surface over to the center of the wheel.

A zero-offset wheel has a mounting surface that's precisely in the middle of the wheel. Move that mounting surface outward, and the result is called a positive offset. Move the mounting surface inward, and it becomes a negative offset. You'll always see offset measurements stated in millimeters.

Backspacing is the third measurement that is needed. It's the distance from that same spot (the back side of the mounting surface) over to the inside lip (or backside) of the wheel. This measurement, for some reason, is made in inches.

There are online calculators that you can use if you want to double-check your math and measurements. Also, most wheel vendors are happy to help you choose wheels that will work well with your Bug. It's important to get wheels that fit your car properly, so you don't end up having your tires rub when you turn or discovering that your wheels won't fit over your brakes.

Popular Wheel Selections

Many types of aftermarket wheels might catch your eye. A popular choice that we see is to use Porsche rims (5/130 mm). There are also stock wheels, of course, if you want to keep the same look but need to replace your existing wheels.

Deep Dish

If you want a more sinister look for your Beetle, consider deep-dish wheels. They're wider than stock wheels and have more area between the outer lip and the spokes.

While this can be a great look, deep-dish wheels may present some performance issues. They have very little backspacing, which changes the way your tires will handle. Specifically, your wheels may stick out farther than they did with a stock setup. This may lead to accidental meetings between your tire and nearby curbs until you learn to adjust your driving.

Split Rim

Another popular wheel choice, especially for Beetle owners who are interested in high performance, is the three-piece wheel, or split rim. They're made of three separate parts: a center, an inner barrel, and an outer barrel or lip. Bug owners who choose three-piece wheels do so because they want a custom fit.

In most cases, these wheels are custom-made to your exact vehicle specifications. If you've lowered your suspension, added bigger brakes, or otherwise modified your car such that mass-produced wheels won't fit right, this is a good solution. You can get them with a custom finish too.

Assuming that you buy new wheels that fit your Bug like a charm, this is one of the fastest, easiest ways to give your ride a look that stands out. Be sure to save your original wheels in case you ever want to go back or if you someday sell your car.

This deep-dish rim deserves some custom-painted hubcaps. You can really set your ride apart with paint. The only limitation is your imagination.

With the availability of a custom retake on the classic Porsche Fuch, it is now possible to do 17- and 19-inch rims under your ride.

BRAKES

Brake failure is the surest way to bring a joyride in your Beetle to a screeching halt. If you've ever driven on a highway that snakes through a mountainous area, you've seen the "last resort" lane. These runaway car and truck escape routes usually sport an ominous set of tire tracks in the deep sand. Someone got going, then physics joined forces with a worn-out brake system to give some poor driver a really bad day. However, it sure could have been worse!

Granted, it's easier to stop a 3,000-pound (or so) Beetle than a semitruck. Plus, if all else fails, a strong tug on your emergency brake should do the trick. However, a big part of classic car ownership and driver responsibility is keeping your car in roadworthy condition so that you can drive it without hurting yourself and others.

While some Beetle modifications and customizations add a lot to the appearance of your ride, this one is more focused on safety. After all, as much fun as it is to go for a drive in your Bug, being able to stop at will is pretty nice too.

Still sporting the original brakes your Beetle rolled off the factory line with? Experiencing some dicey

Disc brakes up front make a nice upgrade from the factory-installed drum brakes. In the back, this upgrade is not as crucial. (Photo Courtesy Bryan Bacon)

Beetles rolled off the factory floor sporting drum brakes all around. The technology of disc brakes is far superior for stopping power and a wise upgrade to make.

moments as you try to stop your car in traffic? How about a little shimmy, shake, and shudder going on when you brake? Or are you noticing that your braking style is best described as "pedal to the metal" lately? All of these symptoms point to the fact that it's probably time to do something about your brakes. There's no better opportunity than now to upgrade.

For anyone with basic mechanical skills, replacing and upgrading your brakes is a pretty easy weekend project. You have a few options, and some will impact other systems in your car. Here is the information and advice that you need to make the best choice for your budget, situation, and design goals.

Why Upgrade Your Brakes?

It all boils down to physics. When your Beetle rolled off the factory line decades ago, it stopped just fine. Even if your Bug was only driven to church and back for its first 50 years and even if it never missed an appointment for routine maintenance, you still need to look at replacing and upgrading your brakes. That's because brake fluid degrades, corrosion sneaks in, and mechanical failures can sneak up.

Now, throw in the possibility that you (or some prior owner) upgraded your engine at some point to keep up with the flow of traffic on today's crazy highways. If your Bug has greater horsepower today than it did when it was built, you need better brakes than it had coming off the line. Bigger, faster engines mean it'll take more to stop that car.

When Beetles were in high production, they came off the line with drum brakes. For a quick visual of how drum brakes work, put this book down for a second and stretch your arms out in opposite directions, as far as you can make them go. Now, stretch them even farther out. Imagine that your hands are pushing against a wheel in motion. The friction will stop that wheel . . . eventually. That's essentially how drum brakes work. Disc brakes, in contrast, essentially squeeze the wheel until it stops spinning.

Innovation is a beautiful thing. Hydraulic drum brakes sure beat their mechanical predecessors, which operated with cables. A sealed hydraulics system uses fluid, levers, and calipers to bring a body in motion to a full stop. This, of course, beats Fred Flintstone's method of dragging his feet to stop his car. Disc brakes take stopping power to new heights entirely.

The One Instance to Keep the Original Drums

The old drum brakes that came standard with Beetles are a great solution only for one type of owner. Keep the drums if you're a purist who is dead set on keeping your ride absolutely true to stock, if you're into matching numbers, or if you're into competing on the concours level.

If you're adding more horsepower to your Beetle, definitely upgrade the brakes as well. Going fast is good. Stopping is even better.

This rear brake drum came in for a rebuild after many miles on the road. Part of routine service for drums in the rear is replacing the shoes and adjusting the emergency brake.

Most likely, you're not driving your Beetle much in this case. You're probably not reaching top speed when you're rolling it in and out of a trailer, so it won't take much to bring it to a full stop.

Collectors who want to preserve their stock cars that are never to be driven or, God forbid, modified play by different rules. However, for most Beetle owners, the point is to actually *drive* your car. Functionality drives a lot of decisions, and there's no more important function than being able to stop at will.

Should you want to take your Beetle off-road, a brake upgrade is an absolute must. The stock setup won't hold up to the aggressive braking that happens when you leave the pavement.

Bare bones safety issues aside, you might decide to upgrade your brakes based on stylistic choices. If you want to change the wheels, the look you want may also mean a change in the bolt pattern. If you change the bolt pattern, you're most likely going to need to change your brake system too. There's always a domino effect when we start tinkering and tweaking.

Classic Volkswagen drivers are nothing if not tinkerers and tweakers. We're always looking for something to rebuild or improve, even if the last project only finished an hour ago. Having a Beetle is like working on a puzzle that takes a lifetime to complete.

Most of your Beetle's stopping power happens in the front of the vehicle. Obviously, with an air-cooled Beetle, the engine's in the back. While that arrangement might sound strange, it works as long as your brakes are regularly maintained, you stay on the pavement, and you

don't swap out your stock engine for one with more teeth.

But if you go off-road, move your fuel tank to the back, get larger tires up front, or install a bigger engine before the fine German engineering goes to pot. The stock front brakes will brake harder than the rears. In the best-case scenario, you make a dramatic entrance, complete with a burned rubber–scented skid. In the worst-case scenario, you don't stop at all.

Beetle Brake Options

When it comes to giving your Beetle stopping power, four basic options are available. The best option for you depends on your budget, how and where you plan to drive your Bug, and how religiously you'd like to adhere to a bone-stock setup.

Stock Brakes

Stock drum brakes are ideal if you're hooked on the classics to the extent that you don't want to modify or customize anything on your Beetle. The same holds true if you're preparing to compete in a concours show. In this case, your whole goal is to restore your Beetle to match exactly the state in which it came from the factory, warts and all. You'll find that brake parts are readily available both used and in new original stock (NOS).

Varga Brakes

Starting in 1970–1971, the Volkswagen factory put spindle and disc brake sets onto all Karmann Ghias. Made by Varga, this setup was a great improvement over the drum brakes that they'd used until then. Some Beetle owners have made the same switch to Vargas and love them.

This 1969 Beetle shows off its Varga brakes, which were standard on Karmann Ghias. They are compatible with Beetles as well.

You can, of course, go to your favorite Volkswagen parts house to buy a spindle and disc brake kit for a Ghia. Or, if you're feeling adventurous, you can just head out to a pick-and-pull junkyard that so happens to have a junked Karmann Ghia on site. As all of these classic Dubs are becoming more valuable by the minute, so, due to limited supply and increasing demand, the pick-and-pull option may be wishful thinking. On the plus side, these are Volkswagen-engineered parts.

EMPI or Scat Brakes

EMPI and Scat both make good disc brake kits that will do nicely as an inexpensive upgrade. The kits are fairly easy to install and will provide good stopping power. There is a drawback that comes with both Varga and EMPI brakes, though. They come with a solid rotor, instead of one with cross-drilling or vents, which means that they won't dissipate heat as efficiently as some of the higher-end kits. But still, both are nice upgrades from drum brakes.

The other concern with these

kits—and it's one that the manufacturer is addressing more effectively than ever—is issues with machining quality. Sometimes, new parts are bad when they come out of the box. You won't necessarily know the parts are bad until you've spent a weekend working on your Bug's brakes, but you'll find out soon enough.

The challenge is that the manufacturer can't check every single part that comes off the factory line. Although, spot-checking is part of the quality assurance protocol, of course. The company has made great strides in its quality over the years, but there's still a possibility that you get a dud. Make sure to examine the new parts when you unbox them. Look for mis-machined areas, warped rotors, uneven surfaces, and tolerances that just aren't right.

You may catch the flaw before installation, but more likely, you'll have your Bug on the road for a test drive before you realize you have a problem. If that happens, just talk with the parts supplier and they'll likely send replacement parts. On the bright side, you'll be twice as experienced in brake installation if you have to redo the work.

Wilwood or CSP Brakes

As always, you get what you pay for when it comes to buying car parts (or pretty much anything, really). This option is rather pricey, typically costing three to four times what you'd spend on the EMPI or Scat kits. Wilwood is a high-end brake manufacturer in Camarillo, California. It doesn't actually make a brake kit for Beetles, though. Theoretically, you could pull together all the parts

This EMPI Wide-5 kit allows the fitment of classic 5 x 205 rims with a disc brake behind it. You'll find this to be a relatively economical choice.

Rear disc brakes can be added to early swing-axle transmissions to increase stopping performance. There are many manufacturers; this one is from EMPI.

 TECH TIP | **Tools Required**

Gather the following tools and equipment to upgrade your brake system (whether you decide to go with drums or discs):
• Impact wrench
• New brake kit
• New brake seals

These are the tools that you'll need for a brake rebuild, including an impact wrench, a socket set, new master cylinder, new brake cylinder, new shoes, and new hardware kit.

Wilwood makes a good high-performance disc brake kit. This kit's rotor has been vented and drilled to dissipate heat faster and stop better.

When installing an aftermarket brake kit, do a mockup to check the clearances. You don't want parts rubbing where they shouldn't.

The impact wrench is not a necessity for removing the lug nuts. However, it makes life easier, and you'll avoid hurting your knuckles.

needed to make your own kit. However, you'd probably need to hire a machine shop to fabricate the brackets needed to attach the calipers.

There is an easier way, though. CoolRydes Customs in San Diego, California; Airkewld in Phoenix, Arizona; and Custom & Speed Parts (CSP) out of Bargteheide, Germany, each recognized the growing demand in the marketplace for ready-made Wilwood disc brake kits and answered the call.

These kits feature calipers, rotors, and other brake components and are available in two- and four-piston configurations. Some of these suppliers drill and vent the rotors for you, which makes it easier to quickly dissipate the heat caused by braking. This perk reduces brake fade while increasing stopping power. Brakes work by turning kinetic energy into thermal energy, so being able to keep the heat to a minimum is kind of important.

Brake Fluid Safety

Other than pinching your fingers, the riskiest part of working on your brakes is the possibility of coming into contact with brake fluid. This substance devours anything it touches, so don't let it touch you.

Never use old brake fluid. The chemical makeup is hydroscopic, which means it absorbs moisture from the air. This absorption leads to contamination, which means it can no longer expand and contract correctly. The end result is brakes you can't trust to work when you need them. Wear gloves when working with items that use brake fluid!

Stock Drum Brakes

If you're a stickler for stock, but you also have a healthy appreciation for the power of being able to stop, swapping out the old drum brakes for new ones will probably sound

like the best option to you. We'd still urge you to consider upgrading to disc brakes, but it's your Beetle, of course.

Original year-correct stock drum brakes are the best choice for Beetle owners who plan to compete in concours shows where these details score points. If this is the way you want to go, follow these instructions to install new drum brakes:

1 Jack the chassis up and take the wheels off. Each wheel is held in place with 17-mm lug bolts. You may need to use an impact wrench to persuade the bolts to turn. Once you remove the wheels, take the rims and tires off too.

2 Reach behind the first brake. You'll find four rubber plugs inserted into the backing plate, and they all need to come off. Two have star adjusters in them. First, back the star adjusters off. That relaxes the brake shoes and eases them off the brake drum. If you've ever adjusted

Having all of your components off, now is a good time to freshen them up. Use a wire wheel first, then paint to help prevent corrosion.

Here's a backing plate with a fresh wheel cylinder installed. The star adjusters are also cleaned up and lubed.

The nice thing about the backing-plate configuration is that it allows you to bench build most of the brakes. Fresh hardware, springs, shoes, and the wheel cylinder are ready to go.

There's a paper gasket that helps keep the wheel bearing oil from leaking onto the brake shoes. If your shoes become contaminated with oil, they will not function properly.

brakes, this process will seem familiar, though backward. Essentially, you are un-adjusting your brakes.

3 After removing the hubcap or bearing cap, you'll see a slip nut with an Allen key that locks it in place. Loosen it and remove the slip nut. Remove the washers and retaining plates, then slide the brake drum off the rotor.

4 Next, the whole brake assembly has to come off the axle. Either cut or unscrew the rubber brake hose. Then, find the retaining bolts around the brake hub and remove them.

5 Work on the brake shoes next, keeping all components intact, such as the springs, star adjusters, hardware, and clips. Clean and polish or paint the parts you'll reuse, including the tension rods, backing plate, and star adjusters. Coat these components with a quick spray of anti-seize.

6 Install a new brake cylinder onto your backing plate by inserting an 8-mm bolt from the backside. Get the new brake shoes loosely in position. Insert the retaining pins and spring through the back, then put the retaining cap and spring on top of the brake shoe. Lock the

The hole in this brand-new rear brake shoe is for adjusting the star adjusters. Before you bolt it up, slide the drum on and adjust the adjusters until they make contact with the shoe. Then, back it off half of a turn.

shoes in place before going any further.

7 Install the upper space slider and spring assembly to the left part of the brake shoe. Then, attach the lower spring set and slider onto the right part of the brake shoe before putting both brake shoes in their proper positions.

8 Place the backing plate onto the spindle and bolt it up. Don't forget the Loctite. Install the bolts again and torque them to the manufacturer's specifications.

Varga Disc Brakes

Bolt the Varga spindles onto the upper and lower ball joints. Prep the rotors by installing and pre-greasing the bearings (both inner and outer). Install the inner and outer bearings. Make sure your inner seal is set in place. Slide the rotor over the spindle. Install the washer and locking tab. Next, install the clamp nut.

The first stage of torque is 15 ft-lbs. Rotate the wheel as you tighten it to take slack out of the bearings. Loosen the clamp nut next, continuing to rotate the tire as you tighten. You should end up with an end play of 0.001 to 0.005. This measurement is essential to getting maximum life from your bearings.

If the calipers aren't preloaded with the shoes, install the shoes into the calipers. Slide the caliper over the rotor and bolt to the spindle. Finally, hook up the brake lines and bleed the brakes, which we'll cover shortly.

EMPI or Scat Brakes

These brake kits come with installation instructions. You might also want to keep a Haynes service manual handy while you work.

Take the rear axle nut and brake drum off first, then remove all brake shoe components. On the wheel cylinder you'll see the brake line and hose. Disconnect them along with the wheel cylinder, backing plate, and bearing seal cap. Keep every part you remove because you may need to use some of them again after you clean and paint or polish them.

On the axle, install the bearing thrust washer, small O-ring, and spacer. Then, install the caliper bracket and large O-ring on the bearing flange. The bearing seal cap is next; use a new seal. Between the bearing cap and caliper bracket, you'll install one gasket. Then, torque the bearing seal cap bolts to 25 ft-lbs before installing the disc brake rotor.

Take the plastic brake pad spreaders off the caliper before installing it with the washer and 10-mm bolts in the kit. The bleeder screw goes on top. Torque to 25 ft-lbs.

Then, reattach the brake line, being careful not to crimp it. You'll find an adapter in the kit that adapts the caliper to the line. If your Beetle has an independent rear suspension, you'll need to furnish your own 30-inch brake lines for this project. They don't come with the kit.

Apply a thread locker to the caliper hardware, then repeat the whole process on the other side of your Beetle. Bleed the brakes to ensure you don't have any brake fluid leaks. Also top off the fluid reservoir. Replace the emergency brake cables, securing them with C-clips. Finally, lower your car, torque the axle nuts to at least 250 ft-lbs, and test the brakes.

Wilwood or CSP Brakes

As with the other brake options, start by disassembling your existing brakes. This is most easily done by jacking your car up, removing the front wheels, and disassembling down to bare spindles. Save all the connectors, as you may need them. Of course, you'll clean, paint, and polish them before reinstalling. If you notice any burrs on the spindle mount faces, remove them.

Install the wheel studs on the hub, then torque to 77 ft-lbs. Make sure you use the right hub stud pattern for your wheels.

A Good Time for New Ball Joints

Disassemble your front drum brakes all the way down to the spindle. Now is a good time to install new ball joints. The extended-articulation ball joints will provide a smoother and safer ride.

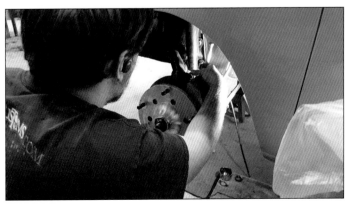

Mount the caliper onto the mounting bracket. Double-check that your caliper is spaced evenly from side to side. You may need a shim to even it out.

Aftermarket Brake Installation

1 *Some high-performance rear disc brake kits come with an internal set of drums for the parking brake. This is a complete assembly, ready for the rotor.*

2 *The emergency brake is installed first. Torque to the manufacturer's specifications. The cable goes through the backing plate.*

3 *The rear emergency brake is bolted down. The next step is to install the emergency brake cable, which is threaded through the rear side of the backing plate.*

4 *We're putting high-temperature bearing grease on the spindle for ease of installation. After packing your bearings, install the oil seal and tap it into place.*

5 *After torquing to the proper specification, there's an Allen bolt that you'll need to tighten on the retaining nut, which clamps the nut onto the spindle threads. This way, you'll maintain correct bearing backlash.*

6 *This is the Mendeola double wishbone suspension. With this kit, the standard camber adjustment nut is eliminated and this machined part goes into the upper side of the spindle.*

7 Loosely fit your upper and lower control arms into the spindle before tightening to spec. After the coilover is installed, the tie-rod end goes into the back of the spindle.

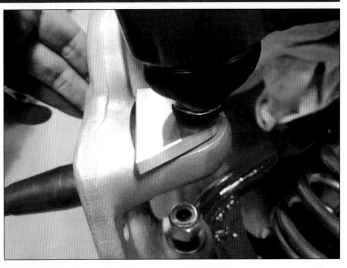

8 After torquing the assembly to the proper specification, do a full range-of-motion check. Make sure there is no binding or interference with the parts.

9 The VW factory used a square hole in the dust cap to drive the speedometer cable. With this kit, you have to install a retainer underneath the dust cap.

10 Notice that there's no hole in the dust cap. Unlike what came from the Volkswagen factory, this is a much cleaner look.

11 The dust cap is simply installed with three screws into the mounting face. Now, it's time to hang the calipers.

Use high-temperature disc brake bearing grease to pack the large inner bearing cone. Install the cone onto the hub's backside. Then, install the grease seal. All you'll need to do is press it onto the backside of the hub, making sure it sits flush with the end of the hub.

Turn the rotor and its adapter and bolt it together. Torque to 25 ft-lbs, following an alternating sequence and using Loctite on the threads as you work.

Next, bolt the rotor assembly onto the hub. Again, follow an alternating sequence and apply Loctite to the threads. Torque to 55 ft-lbs.

Bolt Caliper Bracket

Bolt the caliper mounting bracket onto the spindle. Use a washer and a 0.9-inch spacer between the bracket and spindle face. Then, secure the bolt on the backside of the steering arm with the nut and hand-tighten.

Install the spacer between the spindle and bracket, making sure the flanged heads on the clinch nuts face outward. Hand-tighten the mounting bolts, then install the new hub and rotor assembly. The bracket must align parallel to the rotor. You might need to use shim washers between the spacers and the bracket.

Once you have the bracket alignment right, remove each bolt. Apply Loctite to the threads, re-bolt, then torque the upper bolt to 120 ft-lbs and the lower bolt to 77 ft-lbs.

Turn Attention to Bearings

You'll need to pack the small outer bearing with plenty of high-temperature disk brake bearing grease. Then, install it onto the hub, sliding the rotor assembly onto the spindle. Secure with a spindle washer and the original spindle nut.

Adjust your bearings to meet manufacturer's specs before installing the nut lock (if you have one) and a new cotter pin, which you may need to buy separately. Fasten the dust cup onto the hub.

Mount your brake caliper onto its mounting bracket with bolts and washers. Use two 0.32-inch-thick shims on each bolt between the bracket and caliper. Hand-tighten, then check to ensure the rotor is centered in the caliper.

Adjust if needed by adding more shims (or removing some). You should use the same number of shims with each mounting bolt. The end of each bolt should be flush with its clinch nut. After your clinch nuts and calipers are positioned correctly, start removing bolts. Apply Loctite and reinstall, torquing to 40 ft-lbs.

Don't Forget Brake Pads

Next, it's time to install your brake pads on the caliper. Make sure the backing plates are against the caliper and the friction side is against the rotor. Use a cotter pin to secure. Install the wheel and torque the lug nuts to manufacturer's specs. The wheel should rotate smoothly. Bleed and test your brakes.

Bleeding Brake Lines

Fill the brake reservoir. Starting with the rear passenger-side brakes, work from the outer side inward toward the reservoir. There are two methods that you can follow to bleed your brake lines: get a friend to help you or get a pneumatic bleeder.

With a Friend

Your friend should sit in the car while you do all the hard work. Ask him or her to pump the brakes three times, going all the way to the floor with each push. At the same time, you crack the brake bleeder open to

Pneumatic bleeders make bleeding your brakes a fairly simple one-person job. Hook it up to the shop air to create a vacuum to pull the brake fluid from the reservoir through the brake cylinder to remove old fluid and air bubbles.

If your brake drums get contaminated, you'll have poor brake performance or no brakes at all. Here's what contamination looks like.

When bleeding the brakes, top off the reservoir multiple times. Do not let it go dry. If you do, you'll introduce air into the lines.

exit the brake line. When the bubbles stop, close the valve. You may need to repeat this process several times to get all the air bubbles out.

Brake Component Life Span

Brake lines don't last forever. Over time, they can degrade and become unreliable. Look for any areas with cracks, leaks, moisture, or other damage. Rubber brake lines typically only last 3 to 7 years. If you choose brake drums, you'll need to adjust the drums as they wear out. However, with disc brakes, you only need to replace the brake pads when they wear out.

Being able to stop at will may not feel like an especially exciting accomplishment, but considering the alternative, this project is well worth the effort and expense of an upgrade.

look for air. What you want to see is a steady flow of fluid. You do not want to see air bubbles. You may need to repeat this process several times to get all the air out.

Using a Pneumatic Bleeder

Start by connecting the pneumatic bleeder to the hose. Pressurize the bleeder's canister, then open the bleeder valve. Watch the air bubbles

SUSPENSION

For some Beetle owners, there is no such thing as "too low" on the suspension. Of course, that may mean that rolling over road debris counts as a minor collision.

"Hey, Spook, what do onlookers say when they see a Beetle slammed way down to the ground?"

"I don't know. I'm usually busy driving."

This from the man who put his collection of road reflectors into the shop's display case. He wasn't aiming for them and certainly didn't mean to pry them out of the pavement, but the collection bears witness to one fact: We like our Dubs low and slow.

Of course, we also like them fast. Those two preferences may sound like they're at odds, but they're not, really. If you're driving a slammed vehicle, you just have to realize that railroad crossings, speed bumps, and even loose change that's on the ground (if we're completely honest) are not your friends.

No one really knows who had the first idea to lower their Beetle's suspension. It's a look that's as popular with hot rodders as it is with low-riders. Despite the generally bubbly, friendly look with which Bugs were born, they're remarkably well suited for this much more sinister stance.

However, the trend appears to have become popular in the 1960s. Manufacturers were coming out with air rides that allowed drivers to set

Road reflectors aren't meant to be a showpiece under normal circumstances. But if your Beetle is slung so low that it scrapes them off the pavement, you've earned them.

SCAT Industries makes a fairly inexpensive performance short-throw shifter. You can mix and match your shift knob to go with the theme of your car.

The secret is in the adjusters. With these welded to your beam, you can get the perfect ride height without scraping the bottom of your car.

Upgraded pedals are must-have items if you have feet larger than about a size 10. Note the clutch and brake pedals have a wider format to give you more room.

their cars on the ground when not in motion. The mini-truck fascination of the 1990s brought some advances in suspension setups too. Seeing who could go the lowest became a matter of pride.

However, suspension setups that left cars permanently scraping pavement were impractical and, in many places, illegal. You couldn't pull into your own driveway unless it were completely flat, much less pull into a gas station or get a tow if you needed it. If you got a flat, God help you, because jacking the car up was a major endeavor because of minimal clearance.

Now, the low and slow crowd has it made. With hydraulics, air rides, and racing suspensions, we've never had more options for lowering our cars and still being able to drive them. Of course, once you start tinkering with the suspension, you discover that you've tipped the first domino in a line. Now, you'll need to upgrade a bunch of other parts as well, from pedals to shifters and, of course, narrowing the beam.

If you're considering messing around with your Beetle's stance, here's what you need to know about the options that are available today and how to achieve the low and slow look. As usual, it can be done yourself if you're handy and adventuresome, or you can take it to a qualified shop if you'd rather drop cash to drop it low.

Front Beam Narrowing

You need to narrow the beam before installing any lowered suspension kit. With a narrowed beam,

you gain the necessary wheel clearance to steer correctly. You do not want your tires rubbing your wheel arches. Also, a narrowed beam is pretty cool looking. The narrowed look will coordinate well with the lowered profile.

To get a narrowed beam, you can either do it yourself with some strategic cutting and welding, then fitting beam adjusters on, and bringing the track inward, or you can buy one. If you decide to do it yourself, you'll first need to determine how narrow you want to go. The most popular option is to narrow by 2 to 4 inches, but some builders go way more radical by removing even more material.

Start by disassembling the beam down to its core components, removing the mounting brackets, grease seals, torsion leaves, and outer trailing arm bushings from the beam. Depending on how narrow you want to go, that will determine how much material you will need to remove from the beam. Keep in mind that the narrower you go, the less easily you'll be able to make tight turns.

It's always helpful to build a fixed jig to make sure your welding is straight and true so that you don't end up with a bent beam or misaligned suspension.

Remove half of the amount of the total narrowing that you plan to do out of the section of your beam between the shock towers and body mounts on both sides. For example, if you want to do a 3-inch narrowed beam, remove 1.5 inches out of both the upper and lower torsion tubes on both sides between the shock mount and body mount, yielding a total of 3-inch narrowing. That is about the max you should do on a Standard Beetle beam without having to do significant modifications to the body or the shock mounts.

Next, install your adjusters. Most adjusters come with a new center pumpkin, outer tube, and the adjusters as a unit. It's approximately 1.5 inches wide. Doing one adjuster at a time, go from top to bottom or bottom to top.

Carefully measure, mark, tape, and cut one center section out. Position the new adjuster. Weld the new adjuster into place in the center of the beam. It's very important to maintain plumb, level, and square.

After you finish the first one, do the second one. Never do them at the same time because you're likely to get your beam out of alignment that way. If you reuse the spring pack, reinstall it (you can buy new ones already precut). Put your trailing arms back in. Set your center-positioning pin and jam nut.

Make a mark for the positioning pin and jam nut with a permanent marker. Also, mark on the end of the spring pack where it's sticking out of the trailing arm. Make a mark and cut them off. We find it helpful to use an old trailing arm as a template. Where the centering pin and jam nut go on the trailing arm, drill out some material to create a new cavity for the set pin on the trailing arms.

Take it all back apart. Clean and paint it before installing whatever type of suspension you have in mind.

Airbags, Hydraulics, and Racing Suspension

If you want to start a debate in Dub-land, start talking trash about one of these kinds of suspension modifications. Everyone has an opinion, and you'll hear them all. The "best" suspension choice boils down to your own preferences and driving style. Your wallet has a vote too.

Airbags give drivers high- and low-riding options, but some say the soft handling leaves a lot to be desired. With bags, you might find your car leaning hard to the side as you round a corner and then rolling a bit and leaning harder in the other direction as you exit a curve. Critics say the handling is soft when the car is low and that it is hard and bouncy when it is high.

Hydraulics, on the other hand, solve the soft handling for good. Do you want a firmer ride than airbags provide? You have it. This system is highly responsive and completely customizable when it comes to height. Critics complain about the cost and say that the ride is too bumpy.

Racing suspensions offer higher tolerances, lower production, better engineering, and higher-quality components. They help manage the weight transfer of the car from side to side and back to front. You'll corner like you're on rails and keep constant contact with the road surface so you can go, go, go. However, they are pricey.

Air Ride Suspension

For vintage VW drivetrain components and air ride suspensions, in particular, our go-to expert is Pete Skiba of Airkewld. As Pete explained, static suspensions are fixed at a certain height with no ability to make on-the-fly adjustments from inside the vehicle. It is the "set it and forget it" method. An air ride suspension is the opposite of that. Instead of being stuck in a fixed position, the car can be lifted or lowered with the touch of a button from inside the vehicle.

Air ride on VWs was done in custom one-off configurations in the late 1990s by chop shops and people with the skills and knowledge to make it happen. In 2002, Pete's shop began selling kits after a car show debut at the Pomona, California, fairgrounds. He brought his newly finished 1958

Measure Twice

Measure carefully to make sure everything is level and straight before you go further. Plumb and true is the goal.

Cruising the boulevard. Drop your air ride to low and let the onlookers gawk all they want. While not for everyday driving, this is a great setup for low and slow cruising. (Photo Courtesy Pete Skiba)

With an air ride, you can lay pan fairly easily. This is just one component of this fully customized Beetle. (Photo Courtesy Pete Skiba)

An onboard air compressor with a reservoir tank and controls allows you to lift the vehicle to get into a driveway or onto a trailer or to dodge a cat in the road. Because this suspension system is adjustable, always have the ride height aligned for optimal handling, riding, and proper tire wear.

Some countries do not allow for adjustable suspensions. So, make sure that you ask the right questions of the right people before investing in an air ride.

Knowing how you plan to use the car can provide the right amount of detail and information to make the right suspension system decision for you and your build. If you are building a cruiser (think small engine and small tires) and plan to keep your Beetle under 70 mph, the air ride option is perfect for you. Cruise to your favorite car show, lay it on the ground, and walk away without looking back. Keep it cool.

But if you are building a car with a built engine, maybe even something that might leave some rubber on the ground when shifting to second, this route screams "static suspension." Air ride is more "float like a butterfly," and static is more "sting like a bee."

If you went the air ride route, there are some things to consider. First, choose your wheels carefully. Wheels have diameters, widths, and offsets. The specifics prescribe how you'll need to handle some other matters, such as fender width, narrowed beam, and disc brakes to accommodate the correct bolt pattern.

As Pete describes it, when owners don't take into account all of the specifications that make an air ride work, here's their experience:

Beetle chassis and displayed it for thousands of Dub lovers to see. Since that time, Airkewld has sold 14,000 kits in 49 countries worldwide.

These kits use a combination of air sleeve shocks up front along with torsion bar replacements and air bellow bags with external shocks in the rear. By removing the torsion bars front and rear, the vehicle is now resting on pillows of air. The ride is comfortable and soft.

A nice set of 17-inch rims will fill out your wheel wells nicely. This is a great way to make your ride stand out from the crowd. European-style bumpers are a nice touch. (Photo Courtesy Pete Skiba)

"Your car is done. The air is pumped up all the way to stock height. Your 17-inch Smoothie wheels are shined up. You can't wait to lay the car on the ground with a satisfying *Pssssssssssssss*.

"As your car lowers, you notice that the wheels are sticking out. You can't lower it down. You invested all the time, money, and effort, and it didn't turn out the way you wanted it. Now, you have to do it again.

"But with experience, I could have told you something at the beginning that was *free*, and it would have guided you down a better path and an even bigger smile. I could have told you that with the offset of these wheels, you need to have a 5x205-mm bolt circle with 14-mm lugs. To get that, you need a disc brake kit in that pattern and stud configuration. If you want to lay it all the way down, you will need a 4-inch narrowed beam and drop spindles or 2-inch wider fenders and drop spindles."

So, if you're going to customize your suspension and want to do it yourself the best advice is to talk with the maker of the suspension kit you plan to buy. They work with these systems day in and day out. They know all the right questions to ask about your Beetle so that you wind up with the results you want.

This kit is easy enough to install on your own. However, if you'd rather, you can take it to the professionals. Either send your chassis for rework or they can supply you with a new one. (Photo Courtesy Pete Skiba)

Installation

You absolutely can install your own air ride system, assuming you have basic mechanical skills, can follow instructions, and aren't afraid to call for help if you get stuck. Airkewld and many other suppliers include thorough installation instructions and also provide a helpline that you can call (or email) for additional support.

You'll need three kits to make this work:
• Ball joint kit
• IRS kit
• Air management kit

This guide applies to Beetles manufactured from 1969 to 1979. For other years, the process may be slightly different.

Ball Joint Kit

Use drop spindles with the air ride kit for the maximum drop. Also, if your wheels are close to the fender edge, the fender and fender edge will contact the tire when you install the kit. That's not going to work. Airkewld offers an Ultimate Beam that remedies this problem and makes installation a lot easier.

Loosen the lug nuts a quarter turn before jacking the vehicle up. Then, jack up the front of the car and place stands underneath the chassis. Remove the wheels and place them under the chassis as a fail-safe. Disconnect the battery and remove the dust cap and spindle nuts. Slide the drum off.

On the driver's side, remove the three bolts holding the backing plate onto the spindle. Set them aside. Be careful not to break the brake lines loose so you won't have to bleed the brakes afterward.

Ball Joint Installation

1 Tape off the outer surface where the ball joint installs into the control arms. You don't want to damage the powder-coated or painted finish.

2 Push the ball joint out using a hydraulic press and the appropriate drifts and receivers. Ball joints are under a lot of tension, so be careful.

3 Continue pressing out the ball joint until the drift clears the control arm opening. You may hear a loud pop as it goes.

4 Remove the grease cap from the ball joint. There's a small retainer ring that comes off first. Then, gently remove the boot without damaging the rubber.

5 Confirm correct alignment of the ball joints. This particular front end requires a front-to-back arc.

6 Take the receiver side of the ball joint, flip it over, and then push the ball joint down using the hydraulic press. Use the drift on the bottom to help stabilize the press.

Ball Joint Installation *continued*

7 *Next, install the ball joint grease boot. Slide it on over the shaft. Then, gently pry around the base with a hook to catch the lip.*

8 *Install the retaining clip to the base of the boot. The retaining clip looks like a keychain. You can spread it out gently. Take care not to rip or tear the boot.*

9 *The completed assembly is now ready to go back on the car. With the clips in place on the boot, double-check that the threads are in good shape. Use a die to clean the threads if needed.*

10 *Both upper and lower control arms with ball joints installed are ready to reinstall on the front end. Carefully remove all tape and grease that may be on the units before installing.*

Remove the Spindle

To remove the spindle, loosen the ball joint nuts on the backside of the spindle, but do not remove them. Then, use an air hammer to spring the upper and lower control arms free while avoiding damage to the boots. If you do not have an air hammer, use a heavier hammer to tap the spindle near the ball joint to spring the joints free. Now, remove the nuts.

You can now make a choice. If you want to remove the spindle entirely, you will also need to remove the tie-rod. If you do not, simply swing the spindle out of the way.

Remove the Control Arms

It is time to remove the upper and lower control arms. Remove the jam nuts and the grub screws and slide the arms out. Next, check the ball joints. If there is up-and-down play, it is time to replace the joints.

Remove the center grub screws and remove the factory torsion springs. Then, install the through rods. These inserts allow your front end to move freely. The through rods come in two pieces: one male and one female. Screw them together and add a little Loctite to create a bond. Slide the rods into the front end.

Reinstall the Control Arms

To install the upper and lower control arms, pop the dust caps out of the control arms. A drift/punch and a dead-blow hammer make this easy. If you have an Ultimate Beam from Airkewld, slide the control arms in the beam. If they do not slide in easily, remove them and polish the bearing surfaces to make sure they move freely.

You will need to sand the grooves to get them smooth. If you see major grooving, it's time to replace the bearings. Always remember to use assembly lube for all surfaces as you do the installation. Once all items are moving freely, pump grease through the grease zerks on the front end. Around 10 to 12 pumps will be sufficient. If you did not purchase the beam, slide the supplied Delrin spacers onto the control arms and slide into the beam.

Assembly Required

Install the supplied hardware as follows: washer, thrust bearing, washer, jam nut, jam nut. Tighten all the way down until the arm does not move and back it off a quarter turn. Check to make sure that the washer touching the control arm sits flat. If it doesn't, surface it until it does. Cut the remainder off with a die grinder or a hacksaw, then smooth it out and paint. Make sure the arms rotate freely and smoothly. If they do, you are good to go to the next step.

It is time to install the spindles the opposite of how you removed them. Make sure you lube all the holes where the ball joints go to make adjustments easy. Tighten the ball joint nuts about 70 percent. If you have a level or degree finder, place it on the face of the spindle and rotate the eccentrics until perpendicular to the ground. Now, snug the ball joint nuts. Reinstall the backing plates with the original hardware and tighten. Reinstall the drum/rotor and tighten the nut until it cannot turn

at all. Then, back it off a quarter turn. Install the thrust washer and spindle nut. Reinstall the dust cap, push the speedometer cable through, and attach the original circlip. Trim the lower shock boss so that it is smooth with the bushing.

Air Shocks

Now, install the air shocks with the supplied hardware. With the provided custom fittings, use a thread compound or Teflon tape on the air shock. Do not overtighten the fittings that attach to the air shock because you can split them. Be careful.

These fittings work by inserting a straight-cut piece of tubing into the fitting until it pops into place and then pulls out to engage them. If you need to remove them again, simply push the brass rings in and pull out the tubing.

Run your air lines to a tee and install the inflation stem. Then, do a leak test on the air lines. Please take your time so you will not have a problem in the future. Use a soapy solution on the fittings and fix if necessary.

Reinstall the wheels and remove the jack stands. Make sure the car is inflated so you do not damage your front apron with the floor jack.

Drop It Low

Now, deflate! *Boom!* Your Beetle just hit rock bottom! It is now time to do a "poor man's alignment." Set the ride height to about half of the up-and-down distance. Break your tie-rod-end jam nuts loose.

If you are still running the same beam you had in the vehicle before, center the steering wheel and adjust the tie-rods evenly to keep the steering wheel centered. Measure from one side of the tire to the other. Remember where you measured on the front and back of the tires. Just get it close. Tighten your tie-rod jam nuts.

Independent Rear Suspension Kit

Be safe! Disconnect the battery. Raise the car and put it on jack stands. The higher you lift the vehicle, the easier it will be to install the kit. Be very careful and wear safety goggles!

Independent Rear Suspension Installation

1 *Remove the rear tire and engine for easier access to the rear suspension. Put your car on jack stands for safety. Start by removing the A-arm and axle. Then, unbolt the spring plates. You can leave the axle attached to the transmission.*

Independent Rear Suspension Installation *continued*

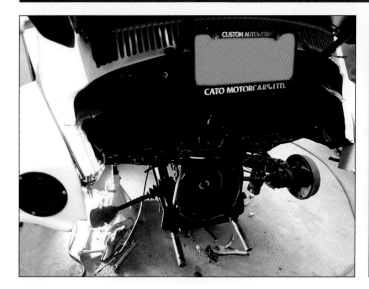

2 With the A-arm removed, hit it with a wire brush and a little bit of Rustoleum paint to protect it. While it's not a part most people will see, it is exposed to the elements.

3 Now that your sub-axles are out (or if you're working with new ones), pre-fit your inner wheel bearing while it's on the bench. You may need to hit it with some fine-grit sandpaper to remove any burrs.

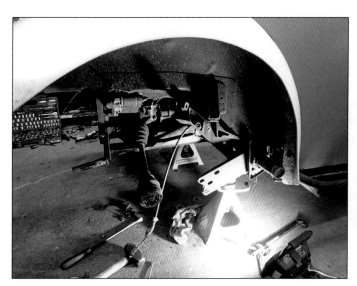

4 While you have all the components out, now is a good time to inspect the fuel lines, control cables, electrical connections, and anything else you can't access when fully assembled. Avoid automotive yoga when you can. If you've raised or lowered your suspension by re-indexing your torsion bars, when you reattach your spring plates, use some Loctite to hold it together. This is a high-vibration area.

5 Polish the half shaft to get the inner race on the wheel bearing to fit better. This will make installation that much easier.

6 It's a good idea to reassemble the A-arms on the bench before reinstalling into the car. This includes the inner and outer wheel bearings, seals, and retaining clips.

7 *With your rebuilt A-arm, it's time to bolt it up. First, slide the inner into the front of the swing arm in its interior pocket. Then, install the shim pack before putting the 17-mm hex-head bolt back in.*

8 *Next, set your shocks in position. This can be done before or after attaching the swing plate to the A-arm.*

9 *Here, we're looking down the A-arm to see that the 17-mm Allen bolt is installed correctly. It should not bind to the right or left side.*

10 *Next, install the three bolts that go from the A-arm to the spring plate. Use Loctite to keep it all in place.*

Remove the rear wheels and disconnect the brake cables inside the vehicle. Remove the four bolts that hold the IRS trailing arm to the spring plate. You will need to reuse these bolts, so don't lose them!

Remove the shock absorber by removing the upper and lower bolts. You will be using this hardware again too. Finally, remove the four bolts holding the spring plate cap.

Using a pry bar, release the tension of the factory torsion bars inside by prying the spring plate off its perch. Be careful because the spring plate is going to spring down extremely fast. It may be better if you stand toward the front of the car and pry underneath it.

Once removed, remove the torsion bar and the rubber doughnuts and set aside. You will no longer need the torsion bars. Do not damage the doughnuts when removing them because you will need to reuse them. If they're worn out, now is a good time to replace them.

Lube As You Go

Lube up the rubber doughnuts with Valvoline grease and install them onto the spring plate. Bolt them using the original hardware. At this time, you can replace them with new rubber versions or you can buy urethane versions. Now, your car will move up and down freely.

Reinstall the original axle bolts and tighten them down. Always use removable Loctite when installing the original bolts. This will give you the peace of mind that they will not come loose on you.

Now, remove the bump stops with a Sawzall or a hacksaw. Once removed, remove the top half of the snubber ball so that it is flush with the trailing arm. Drill a 3/8-inch hole in the center and install the new urethane bump stops.

Tech Shocks

You will now need to install new Doetsch tech shocks. The new shocks have steel spacers inside the box that will need to be pressed into the shock ends. This will allow the shock to be torqued down but does not allow the shock bushing to become smashed. With the old mounting hardware and the 16 spacers included, install the shock and tighten so that they are spaced evenly in the lower pockets.

Grind away the surface paint or undercoating near the upper shock mounts to allow for the welding of the upper airbag mounts. Mount the airbags to the upper mounts as well as the lower bag circles supplied in the kit. You will need to jack up the axle until the shock bottoms out and the trailing arm is hitting the new bump stops.

Trailing Arms

Install the upper mount so that the centers of the trailing arms are just below the upper bag mounts. The angle of the trailing arm and the upper bag mounts must be the same. So, twist the mount until they are the

same. Once everything is lined up, tack the upper mounts in place. Do not fully weld just yet.

With a permanent marker, draw a line around the lower airbag circle onto the IRS trailing arm. This is where you will need to modify the trailing arm by cutting out the circle you just marked on the trailing arm. Once cut out, weld a 3/8 bolt to the lower bag circle. Once welded in, jack the trailing arm up until the bag circle is flush inside the trailing arm and tack.

Test It Out

Check the travel of the control arm by lowering and raising the suspension. Make sure that the airbag does not touch the torsion housing. This will lead to rubbing and may puncture the bag. Once completely satisfied, remove the airbag and weld in the mounts.

Once it has cooled, paint it so it will not rust. Then, reinstall the airbags with the supplied 1/2-inch bushings. Apply a thread compound or Teflon tape to the bushings and install them into the airbags. Insert the 90-degree push-lock fittings into the previously mentioned bushing, and then put Teflon tape onto it.

If you take the time now to leak test them, you will not have problems in the future. Take a soapy solution and spray around the fittings to see if you have a leak. Fix accordingly.

Reinstall your wheels, tires, and E-brake cables, and then let it all down. Make sure you have air in it so you can get the jack out. Now, deflate and watch your jaw drop just as low as your Beetle does.

Air Management Kit

Once you have installed the air ride kits, you're ready to install the

air management kit. There's a debate about the best location for mounting it. There's no right or wrong way, but what follows is how the professionals install this kit.

While the placement varies by Volkswagen model, for a Beetle, we mount it on the chassis Napoleon hat on the opposite side of the master cylinder. With this placement, it can still get air to cool it down, and it is hidden from sight.

Installation Instructions

Place the compressor on the wing and mark or drill the holes. Before fastening the compressor, remove the red rubber plug and screw the supplied air filter into the end of the compressor. Apply Teflon tape to the end of the hose in preparation for a later step. With the hardware provided, fasten all but one of the bolts tight.

Your compressor has two wires coming out of it: a red wire and a black wire. For cleanliness, we like to fasten the ground (black) to one of the mounting holes you just drilled. If you have wire cutters and splicing tools, shorten the wire and tighten the last bolt. Mark, center punch, and drill a hole in the tunnel near the compressor with a 1/4-inch bit. Make sure to open up the hole slightly and deburr the hole.

Relay Installation

To keep the install clean, place the relay in the dash compartment and extend the wires to meet your connections or place it near the compressor. Typically, we do the latter.

If you are doing a high-end build, relocate the relay near your dash. In the supplied hardware pack, you will see a steel 1/4-inch pipe tee, the largest, heaviest fitting in the pack. Once located, you will need to apply Teflon tape to the PSI switch and reducers' connections. Screw it into the fitting in the center location.

On the right side of the upside-down tee, install a 90-degree push-lock fitting without pipe sealant, as it comes applied by the manufacturer. Locate the end of the compressor hose and fasten the line lead into the tee. Adele clamps (not included) help with fastening the tee to the chassis to create an even cleaner look. Hook up the wires per the wiring diagram.

Tank Location

We like to install the tank under the back seat on the opposite side of the battery. For some applications, heater tube modification is needed to place it there. Locate the best position and mark the holes on the chassis. Remove the tank and drill the four holes. Before fastening the tank, install the plugs and fittings into their respective areas.

Since we are only going to use one air outlet, plug all of the remaining outlets with plugs once you have placed Teflon tape on all the threads and tighten. Fasten the tank with the supplied hardware. Locate an area on the chassis where you can drill a 1/4-inch hole for the line coming from the compressor. Mark, center punch, and drill. Don't forget to deburr the hole.

Whether you purchase a 2- or 4-valve air management kit, placement will be the same. The number of lines coming up to the valves will be different. Usually, the valves are mounted in the glove box. Some people have mounted them on the dash or have created a custom mount inside the glove box with fiberglass and wood. But this can be done any-where. Think *clean* when installing them; you will be happier in the end.

Line Placement

Each valve assembly has three line out-fittings: one for each bag or shock per axle and one compressed line. The tee line that goes to the back of the valves is the compressed line. The tees going to the gauges are your shock/bag pressure lines.

When placing a line into a fitting, ensure that the line is cut square. Push the line into the fitting until you hear a click. Then, preload the fitting by trying to pull the line out. This will engage the internal barbs to hold and seal the joint. Make sure to hear the click and try pulling the hose out at every connection.

We like running the lines inside the tunnel for a clean look. It does take a little bit more time to do so, but the end results are a ton cleaner. Installing Airkewld's Inspection Plate Kit, along with removing the shifter and shift coupler inspection plate will make this job a lot easier.

Popular belief holds that if a line passes through a metal hole, the line will rub and eventually create a hole and leak. This is not true. The steel is very thick in the locations that we are drilling, and the line will never move. Installing grommets is not necessary.

Running the lines through the holes might scratch the lines, but they are very thick, and it will not puncture. You will only need to run one compressed line from the tank to the compressor. You will be able to run tees within this line to allow pressure to be run to your valves. When cutting the lines, we recommend a sharp razor blade. The cuts need to be square.

Run a compressed line from the tank to the compressor through the tunnel. On this line, run one line to the valves with a supplied tee. If you are running a 4-valve setup, tee off the line coming up to the valves to have two compressed lines that will

After getting your kit installed, double-check your air management system for leaks. This includes fittings, connectors, and solenoids. A spray bottle of soapy water is your friend. (Photo Courtesy Pete Skiba)

connect to the pressure side of the valves. Now, your entire pressure system can fill and be leak free.

Next, run lines to your bags and shocks. Be clean with your routing of the lines. We like to run the rear lines inside the tunnel again. Connect two or four lines to your bags/shocks and pressure test the system. Use a squirt bottle to apply a soapy water mixture to each joint to check if there is a leak while it is being pressure tested. Lift the vehicle to max height and watch the gauges. If you see a leak in a particular corner, check all the fittings in that area.

Hydraulics

Hydraulics make low-slung cars more drivable. As Ryan Lowther of Demon Motorsports explained, today's hydraulic systems use a stock suspension that can be set to any height. The spring rate is the same as you'd get in a stock suspension. Many say that this is a massive improvement over airbags.

One perk that people love about hydraulics is how you can raise your car to driving height and count on it staying that way as you travel rather than drifting downward as you go. Trying to fix your fittings on the run is not a lot of fun. Also, you won't have to wait for compressors to fill your air tank like you would with airbags. You can even lift your car remotely.

Lest you imagine a lowrider bouncing and hopping down the street, this is not the same thing. Lowriders often use truck springs cut short on each wheel for a super-stiff and bouncy ride. They also run with a trunk full of batteries. With this system, the pump fits under the back seat. You won't even know it's there.

Why use a hydraulic suspension kit? It's one of the easiest ways to get the low look, plus the mechanism is hidden, there are no airbags, and it's an overall cleaner install than you'd get with bags. It's even easier if you can do this modification while your body is off the pan. The price is comparable to airbags (you might spend $6,000 to $8,000 and spend a weekend or two to do it).

Installation

After ordering your kit, inspect it closely and take inventory of the parts received. You'll find templates included in the kit. They'll show you exactly where to cut into the rear torsion housing and the spare tire wheel well if applicable.

Flip the pan over. Then, mark and cut the top of the tunnel just forward of the shift rod coupler access. Be careful not to cut the vehicle identification number (VIN)!

Flip the pan back over. After laying the template out on the bottom side of your pan, mark it and then cut. Remove the center torsion rod housing. The kit comes with replacement plates for added clearance and mounts for the hydros. Weld this in place fully. The front beam is just a bolt-on application. The pump is located under the rear of the driver's seat.

Plumb the lines to the front and rear hydro units. Run the fluid line next. Attach the lines to the tunnel itself or route the lines to the front pump through the inside of the tunnel.

With the hydro kit fully installed and laying pan, you get such a sinister look. Don't worry about the negative camber because you'll raise your ride height when you drive.

The nice thing about laying pan is that when you go to transport your ride for service, all you have to do is bring it all the way up before attaching the lockdown straps. Then, tighten the straps when it's on the trailer.

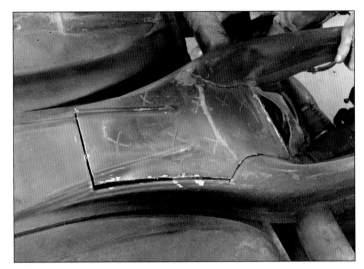

With the templates provided, installation is a snap. Demon Motor Sports templates show you the locations, sizes, and shapes to cut.

Remove the center chunk from the torsion bar housing. Install the new one that comes with your kit.

Be careful cutting the back tunnel. All of the control cables and tubes as well as the fuel line run through this section of the pan.

Front suspensions are pretty much a bolt-on affair. You will have to do a little bit of trimming behind the spare tire, though.

While not cutting off the VIN tag, trim the top of the pan. You need the actuating levers to enjoy a full range of motion.

A compact electric hydraulic pump fits nicely underneath the rear seat, opposite the battery. Everything comes prelabeled and ready to connect.

How low can you go? Tucking some Wide-5 8-inch rims here is no problem. You can get the lip of the rim up to the bottom of the fender.

Next, run your electrical. It's a plug-and-play setup. The guys at Demon Motorsports have done a great job putting these kits together. Don't forget your switches.

Get some fluid in your lines, fill the reservoir, and cycle the system a few times. Then, refill the reservoir, bleed your system, and have fun laying pan!

How low can you go? Well, with this setup, you could smack the ground. You wouldn't do that, but you *could*!

Performance Suspension

Are you harboring secret fantasies about being a race car driver? Do you hate it when your driving abilities far outstrip your car's performance? With a racing suspension, you'll find it easy to hit the apex on your curves and ride like you're on rails.

The CoolRydes Customs lineage of ultra-performance products is famous for its A-arm coilover front and rear kits, formerly only available on Manxter chassis. The suspension provides a better road feel and gives drivers the ultimate in feedback. The components are highly machined with the tightest of tolerances. This is how you bring your old Dub into the 21st century with style.

CoolRydes Customs, owned by Kevin Zagar, bought the rights to the Mendeola design, making it a feasible option for do-it-yourselfers who want the ultimate street machine in their own garage. These are the cream of the crop, and the price tag reflects that excellence.

Performance Suspension Installation

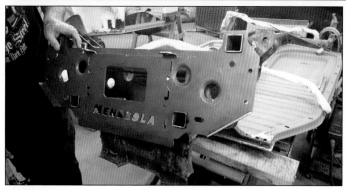

1 *The Mendeola suspension is shipped from the manufacturer as raw steel. Many components will need to be assembled and welded to your chassis.*

2 *The front carrier plate needs to be tapped into place. Leave it loose for now. You will weld it in place later.*

Performance Suspension Installation *continued*

3 You will have to do some trimming on the frame horns. Measure twice and cut once, leaving just a little bit extra. Test fit, mark, then trim with a grinder.

4 The bulkhead support needs to be completely removed for the suspension to fit. Make sure to only remove the bulkhead support and do not cut into the connection between the bulkhead and the lower pan.

5 After all the cutting is complete, do a final dress-up with a right-angle grinder and some 36-grit paper. You want a good, strong, clean weld.

6 Loosely install the front end on the bulkhead. Check for square. Make adjustments as necessary before welding.

7 Get a nice tight fit. You will be marking and cutting off small bits of material from the new bulkhead supports that are attached to the new front end.

8 Don't trim more than about 1/16 inch off the new front end's bulkhead supports. You might need to repeat the process a few times to get a good snug fit.

Performance Suspension Installation *continued*

9 After all the cutting, grinding, and dressing, it's time to clamp it all in place for the final weld up. C-clamps, or compression clamps, will make the job easier.

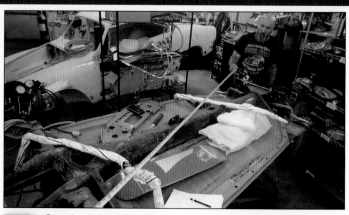

10 One last double-check on the frame for square. Measure from the passenger-side trailing arm support to the top of the shock mount. Repeat from the driver's side to form an X. The measurements should match.

11 Time to start laying some bead. Leave the clamps in place while you weld the support gussets to the frame head.

12 Who doesn't like nickels when laying a good bead? The Mendeola suspension is welded together using tape weld, which is one of the strongest welds out there.

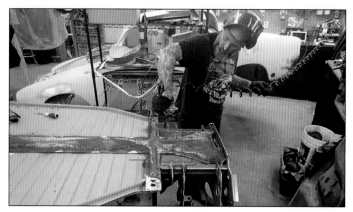

13 After all that welding, you will need to dress your welds a little before continuing. All surfaces must be welded completely.

14 Lower rear sway bar attachment points are approximately 4 inches from the center of the hole to the inside of the rear torsion housing. They are approximately level with the chassis.

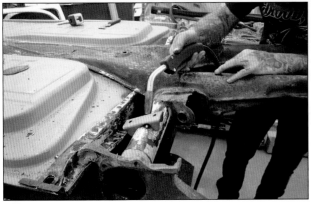

16 With all that hard work on your performance suspension, now it's time to get it powder coated. There are well over 40,000 colors available, so matching your theme is easy.

15 Tack weld in place, then double-check your measurements before fully welding up. You have about 2 to 3 degrees to the horizontal plane of the pan. Make sure both brackets are on the same plane.

17 You will be doing some preassembly work. Lay everything out on a table in the order it will go into your car. That will make your life easier.

18 The kit comes with all-new components. Inner bearing races are installed before the dust cover gets pressed into place.

19 Slide your new stub axles in. There should be almost no lateral play in the stub axles once the bearings and axles are completely seated.

20 One of the nice parts of this kit is its fully adjustable rear end. This eliminates the torsion suspension, but you still need the pivot point for the axles.

Performance Suspension Installation *continued*

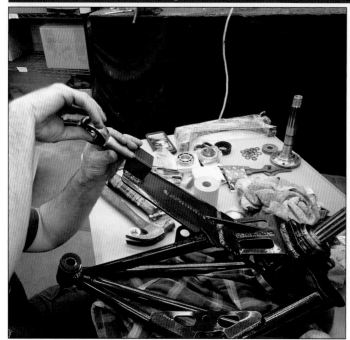

21 The pivot point for the axles is fastened with a heim joint. It simply screws into the trailing arms for a snug fit.

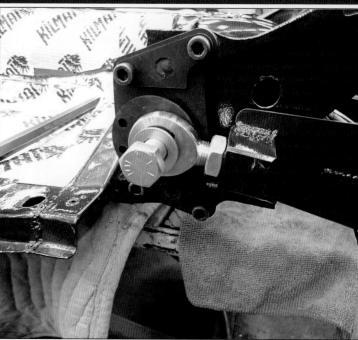

22 Line up the heim joint and slide the retaining bolt through. Torque to spec, and don't forget to use Loctite.

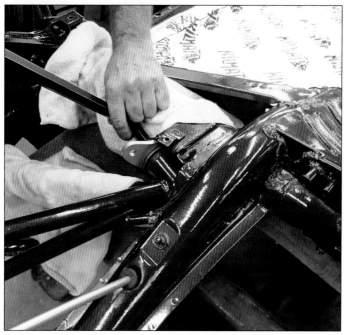

23 The inner pivot point of the rear trailing arm attaches using the original 17-mm Allen-fitted bolt going into the frame horns. If you're using the stiffy bar kit, the tab fits here.

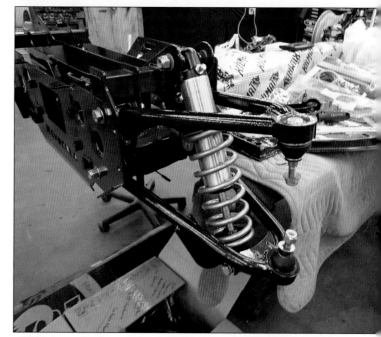

24 You're almost ready to roll; you just need to add spindles, brakes, wheels, and tires. The coilover struts are fully adjustable for ride height and stiffness.

25 This upgraded Kafer bar spreads the torsional load through the entire rear framework of the chassis. All set with clevis and pins, the 1/4-inch plate ties the attachment points together.

26 An upgraded steering rack simply attaches to the brackets you previously welded onto the transmission tunnel. This is a VW rack-and-pinion out of a late-model van.

First, you'll trim the front frame head by 1/4 inch from each side. Remove the bulkhead support on both sides, leaving a 3/4-inch lip all the way around the edge. Test fit the front end.

Dress the edges with a grinder. Some trimming will be needed on the new bulkhead to get it to slide into place properly. Clamp the new bulkhead in place, checking to ensure it is square from shock mount to shock mount. Next, slide the front plate on, then drill out space for the bolts to fit into the bulkhead. Install the four bulkhead screws that came with the kit.

Clean all weld surfaces before reattaching the clamp in place. Check for square again before tack welding the horizontal surface. Then, check for square again before welding your horizontals. After all the horizontals are re-welded, weld the vertical surfaces.

Flip the pan over and weld the bottom frame head in place on the pan. Then, you'll attach the rear sway bar mounts.

Torsion Tubes

Prepare the torsion tubes. Simply locate the mounts so the rear leading edge is perpendicular to the ground, centered on the tubes. Tack weld the brackets in place using the sway bar as a guide for location and proper angles. Remove the sway bar and finish welding the mounts to the torsion tubes.

Install the torsion plates supplied with the kit and tighten the four Allen-head screws. Don't forget to apply some Loctite on the rear swing arms. Install the inner and outer bearings and seal them. Then, install new inner bushings on the trailing arm. Insert the axles and grease well.

Rear Suspension

Set the rear suspension in place. Run the bolt on the torsion plates with washers on each side of the hind joint with the camper cowl behind the washers. Tighten to spec. If you're installing the Tru Track

brackets in place of one of the spacers, install the inner Allen pivot.

After setting the transmission in place, set the Tru Track rear mounts at the transmission mount bolts. Insert the hind joint to the track bar. Note that there are right-hand threads and left-hand threads.

Install the upper brackets tower (top shock to upper track bar) between the shock towers. Then, from the shock tower to the front brackets next to the rear rods. Bolt the strut to the lower A-arm first. Do the same with the upper A-arm. Then, attach the spindle to the upper and lower A-arms. Next, attach the strut (coilover) to the lower A-arm and then the upper A-arm. Torque to spec.

At this point, you can adjust your ride height by adjusting the coilovers with two locking nuts. Next, attach your tie-rods from the steering rack to the spindles. Do a rough adjustment on your alignment. There should be 1/4-inch toe-in front to back.

UNDERHOOD CUSTOMIZATION

When your Beetle first rolled off the factory line, the world's roads were a different place entirely. Speed limits hovered around 55 mph. Interstates were a few lanes wide at the most. It didn't take much to keep up with the flow of traffic. If all you ever do is drive your Beetle out to the ice cream shop in your town, driving only on local roads, you may be perfectly content with "the little engine that could" living in your Bug.

However, if you want to safely drive down the highways and byways

of your world, consider modifying and upgrading your drivetrain. If you have even more daredevil-like plans for your Dub, such as racing it on the track or in a rally race, there's nothing (other than your wallet, most likely) holding you back.

We'll provide some ideas for souping up that Standard or Super, but first, we need to have a heart-to-heart chat about horsepower. In a nutshell, there's a tradeoff for squeezing maximum horsepower out of your engine. You can go, go, go, but you can't do

that forever. The more power you pump through your engine, the shorter its life span will be.

For some Beetle drivers, it's no big deal to replace the engine every few years because they blew it out. But for the more economy-minded owner, you'll probably do better to find the right engine for your particular ride and your specific needs. More is not always better.

We spoke with Steve "Fish" Fisher of Doug's Bugs and Bunnys in Mesa, Arizona, to hear his take on engine

Volkswagen Type 1 engines are not limited to the top-end horsepower of 63. This 1,776-cc engine will produce about 104 hp.

Putting your Bug up on a dynamometer may be disappointing. But seeing as these cars (1969) originally only made 59 hp, it's amazing how much impact a few testing and tuning upgrades can make.

Oil bath air coolers are extremely efficient in keeping particulates out of your airstream. But this was well before the days of cold-air intakes.

Part of the dune buggy's appeal is the availability of aftermarket exhaust and trim packages. This bug guard is more for appearance than function.

This 2,235-cc engine will make 225 hp on the dyno on the rear wheels. For a 1,700-pound car, that is ridiculously powerful.

With performance upgrades, suspension upgrades are necessary too. You want the horsepower to be able to plant the tires.

modifications for Beetles. Fish has seen a pattern in customers seeking bigger engines. They start by wanting a 1,600-cc dual-port engine from a 1970s model to replace the engine in their 1960s Bugs. They'll easily reach 65 to 70 mph.

However, in many places, even that isn't nearly fast enough to safely share the road with modern vehicles. Fish has seen customers put these engines into Volkswagen buses to boost reliability for far-flung trips with the extra weight of a family's camping gear on board.

In a Beetle, this engine can be tuned for high performance. It may also be a good choice for dune buggies, kit cars, and sand rails. You can have an engine built in various configurations to perform well for your intended applications, but an engine's outer limits are worth respecting. If you push it too far, it will run hot until it dies a sad, smoky death. Just as a 350 engine in a Corvette is not the same 350 that's in a tow truck, it's wise to build an engine that aligns with the application into which it's going.

If you're modifying your Beetle to make it more of a hot rod, look into adding more cooling, excellent filtration (and be prepared to replace your filter with every oil change to keep it clean and your engine reliable), and external coolers.

With increased horsepower, you get a cascade effect. Consider upgrading the brakes, the driveline, and the suspension.

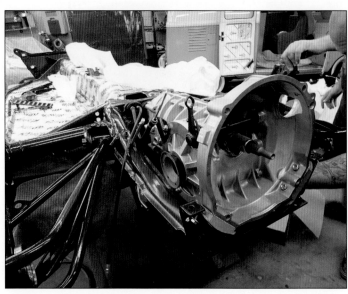

Do not forget to upgrade your transmission to go with the increased horsepower. If this magic box fails, you'll be stuck on the side of the road.

The more you can pour into your engine budget with high-quality parts, the more performance you can expect. Wise engine buying is not just about buying a large engine. While you can certainly drop a lot of money on an engine, be careful not to let it eat your entire customization budget. You can go with a smaller engine that performs bigger if you budget wisely. Choose better parts, including cylinder heads, and you'll get an engine that works well for your purposes and lasts a long time.

Also remember that when a bigger engine is added, you tip over the first tile in a line of dominoes. A bigger engine may require an upgraded transmission, better brakes, and so on.

Turbocharging

As Fish says regarding turbo engines, "Once you go turbo, you never come back." You'll receive great performance from a turbo system. However, it will also reveal any flaws and weak links in your drivetrain. Installing a turbo reveals all of the sins in your system.

It's best to consider this, and your budget, before making that bold move. Turbos are a fairly common upgrade for Beetles.

Supercharging

Superchargers are less common but accomplish roughly the same goal as a turbo. A supercharger compresses air and forces it through the engine, giving a massive power boost. That sounds great, but you need to know about the downsides too.

Superchargers tend to cost a lot more, typically require a professional to install, and reduce your Bug's fuel economy dramatically. They also place a burden on the other components of your Beetle, from the tires to the brakes and suspension. Your Beetle will run fast, but you probably won't be passing it down to your kids and grandkids.

Ways to Upgrade

When it comes to upgrading your engine, there are three common routes you could go.

Build It Yourself

If you're mechanically inclined or brave, and you have more time than money to devote to your project, you might enjoy doing the work yourself. There is no better learning experience than getting yourself elbow-deep in the workings of your engine. You may need to borrow or buy some specialty tools to get the job done. You'll also likely need to find a machine shop that can do the machining work for you.

It's satisfying to perform the work yourself, but as any do-it-yourselfer will attest, you must also be prepared to find yourself on the side of the road. It's all a learning experience.

Hire a Professional

If building it yourself sounds like more of a hassle than an adventure, you can take your Beetle to a shop. Be sure to choose one that has loads of experience working on air-cooled vehicles. Check their references. Get your agreement in writing.

In Fish's case, he builds about 50 engines a year and devotes a significant amount of time to research and development so that he can test and tweak them for maximum performance.

Buy a Kit

Between the previous two options, there is another road you can take, assuming that you are mechanically inclined and up for spending some time tinkering on your Beetle. You could buy a kit and install it yourself.

Most parts suppliers (especially if they sell a ready-to-go kit) are happy to help their customers through the process. Just be sure to have a conversation with your supplier about your project so that you can get exactly what you need.

Short of replacing your engine, there are other ways to modify the drivetrain to add more zip, boost your safety, and get overall better performance from your Beetle. We'll discuss how to increase horsepower, improve airflow, upgrade the ignition and exhaust systems, add some crucial safety upgrades, and even add rocker ratios to get the most from your engine. Let's go!

Horsepower

Beetles are known for their iconic shape, their status as the most-produced vehicle of all time, and the nostalgia that they evoke on sight. They're not typically known as high-performance vehicles with impressive horsepower. However,

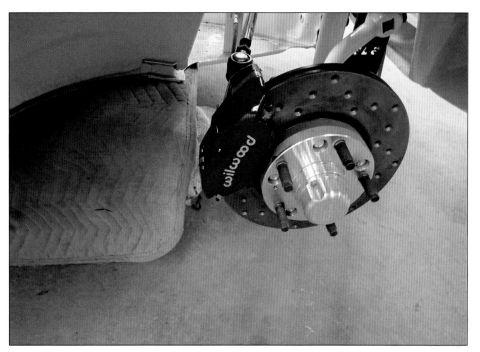

It's always recommended to upgrade your brakes when adding more power to your Volkswagen. Chapter 3 is devoted entirely to upgrading your brakes.

as evidenced by their popularity on drag racing strips, some Beetles have more horsepower than the Germans ever intended.

Intake

Increasing your horsepower begins by replacing the cold-air intake system that came from the factory with a high-performance cold-air intake system. The idea is to let more air into the engine. This is a rather simple swap to make, and the only significant downside (assuming you don't go too crazy) is a bit more engine noise.

Exhaust

The next phase of horsepower boosting involves swapping the factory-built exhaust system for a high-performance exhaust system. This boosts horsepower because it allows the hot air in the engine bay to escape more efficiently. As a bonus, your engine will sound a bit more aggressive when you rev it. If

you decide to change your exhaust system, check with your state's laws first. Some states ban performance exhaust systems because of the increase in carbon dioxide emissions that they cause.

If you want your Beetle to have a throatier sound and possibly increase horsepower (or if you just want the look of a custom exhaust system), this may be the project for you. There are many options, including Fat Boy Mufflers, jet-coated mufflers with better thermal transfer, and balanced and tuned exhausts that yield better engine performance.

The process is roughly the same, no matter your selection. Remove the original exhaust system and then install the new one. There are two nuts at each head on the forward bank, two nuts and bolts on the heater boxes, and a set of donut clamps on the downstream side of the heater boxes and on each of the peasshooter tailpipes.

It might not seem like much, but a cold-air intake can increase horse-power by 3 to 5 percent. That means even a small engine can go deceivingly faster.

While factory-style exhausts from the major manufacturers will do just fine, you might want to look at the stainless-steel options. Many come from Japan, and the manufacturing is dead-nut straight. Plus, they sound good.

If you remove the heater boxes, take the system all the way apart back to the head. If you're keeping the heater boxes, leave them attached to the head and remove the donut clamps at the rear of the heater. Simply bolt up your performance exhaust using new exhaust gaskets and go.

After planing the flanges on the exhaust manifold, do a mockup fit to make sure everything is working correctly. Check for exhaust leaks now too.

Electronic Ignition

You won't see a huge increase in power by making this modification, but replacing your points and condenser with an electronic ignition will help you spend less time on maintenance. You'll also appreciate having a Beetle that starts easily even if the weather is nasty. Installing this device might take just a few minutes, and it's a project that's perfect for the less mechanically inclined among us.

Electronic Ignition Installation

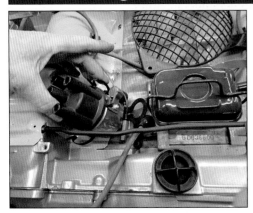

1 *Remove the distributor cap by popping the two tension clips on either side.*

2 *Pull the rotor. Set it aside and keep it in a clean environment until it's time to reassemble.*

3 *You'll see a Phillips or a flathead screw attaching the points to the distributor.*

4 *Remove the screw and pull the points. Disconnect the electrical connections.*

5 *It's just a matter of slipping the halo onto the rotor button in the electronic pickup. Now is a good time to upgrade your coil as well.*

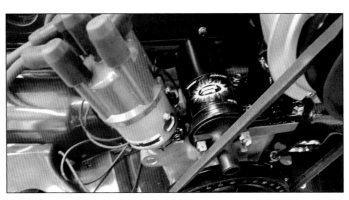

6 *With everything installed, red goes to positive and black goes to negative on your coil. Do not reverse them or you will fry your electronic ignition.*

Here's how to do it. First, disconnect the battery any time that you're working on an electrical system. It's the safe way to work. Release the distributor cap and leave it off to the side with the wires attached. Remove the rotor by pulling it straight up and out.

Now, if you look down in the distributor body, you'll see a single standard screw attaching the points to the distributor body. There's also one electrical connection to the coil. Remove the screw and unplug that wire. Then, remove the unit.

Take the electronic ignition and thread the two wires back through the wire hole. Screw the electronic pickup back down into the same point where you removed the screws. Make sure to connect the positive and negative to the coil correctly. If you reverse them, you will fry the unit. Put the rotor back on, replace the distributor cap, and secure it. You're good to go.

Upgrading your distributor is a small project that yields big results.

There are a few options for upgrades. Bring your engine's number-1 cylinder to top dead center (TDC). Use a permanent marker to mark from the base of the distributor body to the engine case, lining up with where the rotor is pointed for TDC. This will help you later to get a fairly close timing mark.

Remove the wires from the cap, marking each wire for the corresponding cylinder. There is a 13-mm nut holding the distributor clamp down. It's attached to a stud in the case. Gently pull the distributor straight up and out of the engine case.

Install the performance distributor by reversing the process you just used to remove it. Any time you perform ignition and timing work, always recheck the timing of your engine. Each distributor manufacturer provides a baseline timing instruction in the package. One size does not fit all. You may need to adjust a bit for your particular engine.

Fuel System

There are two different types of fuel delivery systems. From the Volkswagen factory, you received a system with a single carburetor. Different carburetors went into different-sized engines in different years.

In the early 1970s, the factory began installing an electronic fuel-injection system (EFI). You won't see many of those original EFIs around anymore because they were extremely susceptible to vacuum links and voltage mishaps. They were great when they were working correctly. Now, many have switched to carburetors instead of continuing to baby the EFI systems.

In the aftermarket, you can select a performance 2-barrel carburetor with a matching intake into the cylinders or you can choose dual carburetors. For Volkswagen owners today, the Baby Weber (an ITC34) is the most common. The other common option is the DLRA, a larger carburetor that can be jetted and tuned for

Mallory makes a drop-in replacement with an electronic ignition. It helps a Volkswagen engine run at optimal performance levels. They are pricey but worth the investment.

The halo pickup is integral to the electronic distributor component. It gives input as to where the engine is within its cycle.

Italian ITCs (Baby Webers) are one of the most common upgrade customizations for dual carburetors. They're good for any engine under 1,835 cc.

DLRAs are also a Weber carburetor. Generally, the venturis are set at 40 ml and are good for engines 1,835 cc and larger. They can be tuned to the engine. Just remember it's one carburetor per cylinder.

If fuel injection is your thing, CB Performance and a host of other manufacturers are making direct-injection manifold systems. They're great for an air-cooled Volkswagen.

Twin forties are always a blast on your ride. Make sure you tune them and have them jetted correctly for your engine and elevation. Otherwise, they will fall on their faces. This is a true performance carburetor.

smaller engines. There's also a third option that's worth mentioning. Several companies make EFI systems for high-performance engines, which are completely tunable on the fly via a smartphone app. The pricing for that system is not for the faint of heart.

It is much easier to perform this upgrade on the bench than in the car. With any carburetor upgrade, you will need to remove the original fuel system, which includes the carburetor intake manifold, intake boots, and end-cap castings. You'll also need to clean up the intake manifold gasket.

Once everything is disassembled for the fuel system, if you're doing a single 2-barrel carburetor, replace your center pipe, carburetor mount, and carburetor. Use your existing end castings with a new manifold gasket and boots.

If you are installing the ITC34 or DLRA, remove the existing system. The intake casting is now your carburetor mount. It is attached to the head with a new gasket. File your mounting surfaces flat and then clean them before installing to ensure a good,

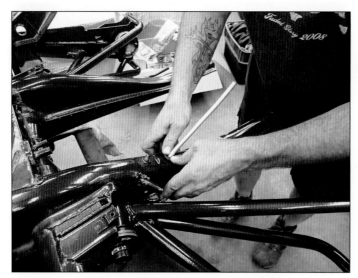

We generally replace the main fuel line going from 5 mm to 3/8 inch. The fuel filter needs to be relocated outside the engine bay for safety.

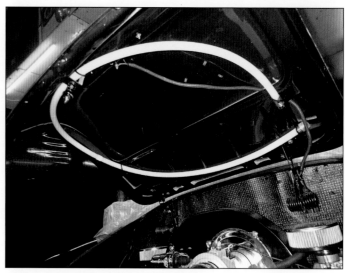

Fire is not your friend. Automatic fire suppression systems are readily available, fairly inexpensive, and highly recommended.

snug fit. Bolt the carburetors into the intake manifold. The EFI installs the same way as the carburetors do. It's basically a plug-and-play operation. Just follow the instructions that come with your specific kit.

There are options for linkages, but the standard for these engines is a hex-bar cross linkage. Each carburetor kit is a bit different. Please follow the manufacturer's instructions included in your kit. You will need to do some tuning on your engine, which may involve re-jetting the carburetors. But if you talk with the company from which you're buying and inform the company of your application and engine size, it can usually pre-jet for your specifications. Although, you will still have to do some fine-tuning after installation.

Fire Suppression

Going fast is well and good, but preventing your Beetle from catching fire is even better. While this is more of a safety measure than an upgrade, it's worth mentioning. Your fuel filter should not be located in the engine bay. Instead, place it where it will come out of the transmission tunnel before it gets into the engine bay or underneath the fuel tank.

While carrying a fire extinguisher in your Beetle is smart, you would have to have lightning-fast reflexes to activate it in an emergency. A better alternative is to install an automatic fire suppression system. You'll install it in your engine bay as a standalone passive unit.

When the engine bay reaches a certain temperature, tubes filled with fire retardant will break and release the chemicals into your engine bay to suppress the fire. Your engine will need to be cleaned if the system ever deploys, but that is a lot cheaper than replacing your engine, losing your car, or endangering yourself and your passengers.

Ratio Rockers

Your engine is, at its most basic, a giant air pump. The more air you put in and the more air you get out, the more power you make. Ratio rockers are an inexpensive upgrade to get a little more juice out of your engine. They change the factory's valve geometry to increase lift and duration in the valves. It's almost like getting a little bit bigger cam without opening your engine up.

You can buy ratio rockers at a Volkswagen supply house. We advise against buying the cheapest rockers available; you'll get much better results by spending a bit more. The better kits also include step-by-step instructions for installation. You can buy them preassembled and ready to bolt in or you can buy just the ratio rockers (you'll need eight) and do the switch-out onto the rocker arms on the engine. Either way, be sure to adjust your valves after installing.

The great thing about these engine modifications is that you can do them gradually, as your budget allows. By customizing these systems in your Beetle, you can improve its safety and performance and keep it on the road longer.

INTERIOR

Now that you're elbow deep in customizing your Beetle, it's time to point out a matter of injustice. How is it right that bystanders and onlookers are the only ones who get to feast their eyes on the beauty of your Dub as it drives by with all its jaw-dropping exterior modifications?

It's not right. Especially when you consider that from the inside of your ride, you might not even be able to see many of the personalized touches you've made. Why shouldn't the interior be just as representative of your preferences as the outside is?

That ends here and now. If our home is our castle, our cars are our home away from home. It makes sense that we'd want to make them reflective of our style, use, and preferences.

This chapter is all about modifications that you can make to your Beetle's interior. We'll explore some popular options and go deep on the installation process that you'll follow if you choose these custom touches. Some upgrades take only seconds to accomplish. Others may prove to be a test of your patience and skills. The financial investment for each option varies greatly, but you can always make a wish list to keep on hand; just cross each improvement off the list as you get to it.

Customization

Car interior customizations have been around at least as long as the urge to modify the exterior. In fact, reports exist of car enthusiasts modifying their Model T and A Fords as early as the 1930s. However, in reality, the modifications probably started about five minutes after the first car owners took delivery.

Granted, the upholstery in the first cars closely resembled the cushions featured on fine furniture with tufted leather and stuffed with horsehair and cotton. Floor mats were woven from cocoa plants for durability, or you can go with a simple rubber mat.

If your Beetle still has its original interior, you know the distinctive smell and feel of the horse hair

While stock upholstery is very nice, with a little time, effort, and imagination, you can level up a notch. From the red stitching to the embroidery on the back-rest, this is a full-custom job.

featured in our rides. Of course, no actual horses were harmed in the making of these seats. Countless coconuts paid the ultimate price for our comfort, however. The seats are stuffed with pads made out of coconut shell fiber.

Aside from recovering their Beetle's seats, the range of more involved interior modifications extends to swapping the seats out entirely; covering surfaces from dash to door with other fabrics; upgrading gauges, knobs, shifters, steering wheels, mirrors, and lights; and even adding high-quality sound systems. Of course, for many Beetle lovers, there is no song quite as sweet as the hum of their well-tuned engine.

The range of possibilities for interior modifications is truly limited only by budget constraints and imagination. However, adding modern amenities like rearview cameras, airbags, video screens, and refrigerators may take some doing. With no computer on board, Beetles are the perfect vehicle for post-apocalyptic times or for cruising around after an electromagnetic pulse knocks all the modern computer-reliant cars offline. However, the absence of a computer makes some custom features quite a bit more challenging to accomplish. With an unlimited budget, there is undoubtedly a way to do just about anything your mind can imagine.

We'll stick to the interior customizations that make sense for most classic Volkswagen owners. Again, there's a major fork in the road that will determine where you go with customizing your Beetle. If you're fanatical about keeping it bone stock (the way that it rolled off the factory assembly line), what you want is not really custom touches—it's more about restoring what you already have.

If that's the case for you and you want to handle restoring your Bug yourself, you might want to check out CarTech's *How to Restore Your Volkswagen Beetle*. But, assuming you're here to find out about the range of modification and customization options you might want to consider, let's talk design principles first.

Design Principles

It doesn't matter what kind of look you're after, there's one guiding principle behind custom automotive design. As you look over the vehicle inside or out, you don't want the flow to be interrupted by something that sticks out, demanding your attention. If your eyes land on any component in particular, it's likely that it doesn't belong there. Granted, this is *your* Bug and nobody else's. You should do exactly what pleases you. However, if you want a professional car designer's philosophy, uninterrupted visual flow is the core principle.

Assuming that you don't have a degree in textile arts or automotive design and that you don't have access to some fancy design software, you may be wondering how to come up with a cohesive plan for upgrading your interior. There's a low-tech way you can play around with your interior without spending a fortune or giving yourself a headache. Just as your average teenager tries on 17

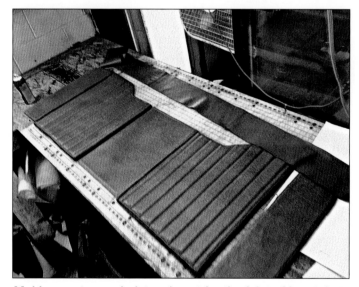

Making custom upholstery is not for the faint of heart, but it is doable. There's a wide range of materials available, including this hand-dyed Italian leather.

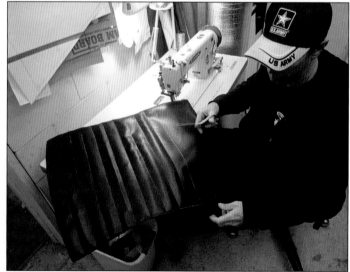

When working with natural hides, you only get one shot to do it right. Each needle piercing stays forever, unlike with fabric. Leather never heals.

If you want to upgrade the back seat to make napping or camping remotely comfortable, you can. It'll just take a little bit of cutting, welding, and a whole lot of cushion.

One of the easiest ways to customize your Beetle's interior is to create an emblem all your own. You could even have it stitched into custom seat covers for a quick modification.

outfits before settling on one to wear for the day, there's a simple process that you can follow to test infinite design ideas before selecting one.

Essentially, all that is needed is to take pictures of the inside of your car. Do this from many different angles, making sure to capture every element you might want to modify. They don't all have to be in the same shot, of course. Print some of your clearest photos. Then, trace them onto plain paper, creating detailed line drawings of the interior features. It may be easiest to tape your photo covered by a sheet of plain white paper onto a window so that the sunlight makes it easy to trace.

Then, make multiple copies, saving the original in case you need to make more. Use these copies to play around with your design. You can test out infinite color combinations, patterns, textures, and shapes. This process sure beats testing your ideas with real and expensive elements.

Make, Buy New, or Custom-Made?

Just as there are some basic customization routes you could follow for the body and mechanicals of your car, those same options apply to modifying your interior. You can make your own, order off the rack at a Volkswagen parts house, or buy custom options made just for you.

Not many Beetle owners are masterful upholsterers, so the option of sewing your own may not be practical. It's not even a matter of having decent sewing skills. The materials used for upholstery are different from those used for making clothing. They're expensive, especially if you choose leather or suede. With these materials, you get just one shot as you sew.

Unlike some fabrics that "self-heal" as you sew, if your needle punctures the hide, you have a hole. Better hope it's in the right place! The second significant difference between sewing clothing and upholstery is equipment. You'd need an industrial-strength sewing machine with appropriate needles. Otherwise, your poor little Singer will die a premature death. Home sewing machines just can't withstand the beating they'll get taking on an auto-

motive upholstery project. If you decide to make your own interior, CarTech's book *Automotive Upholstery & Interior Restorations* would be a wise investment.

Assuming that the do-it-yourself option is impractical for you, your remaining options are buying kits to install on your own or taking your Beetle to a shop that specializes in custom interiors. You can probably guess which is the more economical option. Professional custom work is pricey. However, your list of options becomes virtually unlimited if you go that route. Want buttery-soft, two-toned ostrich leather seats? No problem, as long as you have a small fortune you can spend to get them custom-made and installed.

But for most of us, the most feasible way to customize an automotive interior is to look at the options available off the shelf at your favorite Volkswagen parts houses, manufacturers, or smaller suppliers. If you're planning an upgrade, one of the best ways to discover the many options available is to visit a trade show. There, you can see, touch, smell, and

A benefit of using synthetic leather or vinyl is that you have a wide range of colors available. You can match your color scheme to a tee.

Synthetic leather gives a luxurious feel, like you'd get with a much more expensive material. They're also extremely durable and easy to work with because they self-heal.

even sit on or otherwise test drive any products that catch your fancy.

Fabric

Visit a car show and you're likely to see all kinds of creative upholstery. From burlap coffee bags and Mexican blanket–covered seats to license plate–covered door panels, denim, and even highly impractical but fancy satin touches, we Beetle lovers are an inventive bunch.

Excluding those especially inventive fabric choices, there are some basic options to consider. Your budget will help you decide. However, a point we can't repeat frequently enough is that it's always wise to buy the best you can afford. Durability matters, so consider how various materials will wear and how they'll hold up to UV light. Mixing and matching is always an option as well and can greatly multiply your stylistic options.

Vinyl

Vinyl is one of the most durable and versatile materials ever invented. It stands up well to spills and dirt. Manufacturers can produce vinyl fabric that's velvety soft or burlap rough. The price you'll pay for all

that ruggedness is that, in the end, vinyl is essentially plastic. It won't match your body temperature when you sit on it, so what is gained in durability is sacrificed in comfort and luxury.

Faux Leather

Made from vinyl or microfiber, faux leather lands on the next rung of the upholstery ladder. Highly versatile, this material can be made to look like any number of higher-end materials. Want snakeskin seats? How about a crocodile skin–covered steering wheel? Colors or patterns? Also want to be able to wipe these surfaces clean with a damp cloth? Faux leather may be just the ticket. You'll get all the durability and stain resistance you'd get from plain vinyl

plus the style points you'd get from animal hides.

Leather

So buttery soft that you'll probably lose track of time stroking it, leather is an option that'll cost a pretty penny. But every time you get into your Beetle and fill your nostrils with the scent of leather, you'll be glad you found a way to get this upgrade for your ride. There's nothing finer than smooth,

Leather is, by far, one of the hardest products to work with and get it right the first time. However, you'll get maximum durability as well as a luxurious feel.

glamorous leather. In fact, it may be the perfect choice for automotive upholstery.

As long as you take care of it, leather can last a lifetime. A natural material, it grows softer with use, adjusts to your body temperature, and looks gorgeous for decades—even when it takes on a bit of patina from extended use.

Suede

It doesn't get more sensual than suede. This "fuzzy" leather has a napped finish you may find yourself rubbing just to make it stand up and then lie down. Of course, if your passenger spills a Coke in your suede-upholstered Beetle, matters can get dicey fast.

Unless you treat your suede with a specially designed fabric protector and clean spills immediately, they will soak in and ruin the hide. Go this route, and it would make sense to carry a suede cleaning kit in your glove box. Blot, brush, and dry is the basic process you'll need to practice if you want to keep your suede looking like new.

Tweed

If you have spill-prone friends and don't want to enforce a beverage ban in your Beetle, tweed may be the upholstery material for you. Highly versatile, tweed wears well, and compared with suede, it cleans more easily.

You can get tweed in various patterns and colors, including tartans and other plaids. It's also relatively easy to work with because it stretches well on the warp (vertical) and weft (horizontal) axes. However, all that utility comes at a price. Tweed is not especially comfortable; in fact, "scratchy" is the first word that comes to mind. While it's easier to clean than suede, it's not effortless to keep clean, and it won't hold up to vigorous scrubbing.

Not only can you choose brand-new seat covers in any of the materials we just discussed, but you can also replace the entire seat by removing yours and bolting new ones in. This may be a good choice for Beetle drivers who want more ergonomic seating or who find that the original seats just don't fit their frames comfortably.

Seat Recovering

If you want to simply recover your seats, now is also a good time to do a little bit of restoration work to repair any damage the years have done. After you strip the covers off, send the frames out to a sandblasting company. When the frames come back, you'll be able to see

Tools Required

Gather the following tools and equipment:

- Hog ring pliers
- Hog rings (one package)
- Bailing wire
- Hair dryer (for vinyl seats)
- Jute (about 4 to 5 yards for one Beetle)
- Upholstery shears
- Foam
- Roll of plastic wrap
- Pliers
- Small hammer
- White grease

Vinyl was one of the most common fabrics applied to Beetle seats. It's easy to clean, durable, and looks at home in your Bug.

Tweed is an excellent choice for automotive upholstery. It's not quite as comfortable to the touch as leather, but it's exceptionally durable.

where any repairs are needed and whether broken springs or dents are in the frame. Now is a great time to give the steel some rust protection by spraying it with a coat of paint.

Once the paint dries, wrap your frames in jute. This will help keep the springs where they belong rather than poking your kidneys while you drive. Foam or horsehair cushions come next, depending on whether you want to stick to stock or go for a potentially more comfortable and less "original fragrance" option. Painted, jute-wrapped, and cushioned, all you'd still need to do is install your new covers.

Seat Recovering

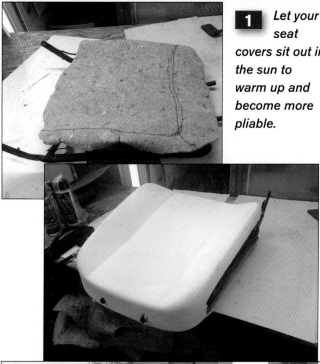

1 Let your seat covers sit out in the sun to warm up and become more pliable.

2 Cut the jute to fit your seat frames. Attach to the frames using the hog rings.

3 Clean with a pressure washer, do a media blast to strip it, repair, and repaint your seat frames with Rustoleum spray paint or powder coat.

4 Cover the jute with a layer of foam. Wrap the foam with packing wrap or plastic wrap. The plastic's slick surface will make finessing the covers into place a lot easier, almost like you've added lubrication.

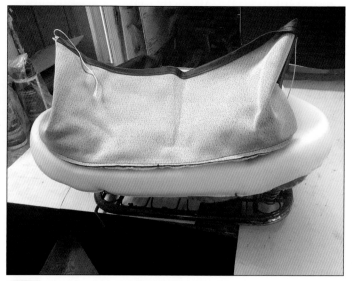

5 You'll notice that your new seat covers have cloth hold-down ties. Replace those ties with baling wire to make them more durable.

Seat Recovering *continued*

6 *Slide your new covers on over the foam and plastic wrap. It's easiest to work from the front to the back. All you need is a loose fitting this time around. Pay attention to the seam placement to get the covers on straight.*

7 *Flip the base over and begin pulling the seat cover's hem around the lower frame. You'll see some spikes under the frame. They're meant to anchor the seat covers in place. You'll also see metal tabs on the under-side. Hammer them flat after your seat covers are where you want them. Get the tab edges flat.*

You'll need a super-sharp pair of scissors for cutting jute. Jute is made from recycled materials and has heavy cross-link fibers, but it's crucial for preventing damage from a sharp piece of metal from the frame. New foam is readily available from your Volkswagen parts supplier. It's denser and far more comfortable than the original coconut fiber.

The precut foam you bought for your project is shaped to the seat. It's nearly foolproof to install. A quality foam is quite a bit thicker than the original.

Some of the less expensive kits use string for the rear hold-downs. We prefer to insert a wire rod into the bottom pocket to more closely match the original factory fit. It's always a good idea to warm your vinyl first by setting it in the sun to soften a bit. By turning them inside out, you'll have an easier time installing them. We find it easiest if you compress the springs and foam while attaching the seat components to the metal tabs.

Get a Helping Hand

You may want to ask a friend to help with your seat-recovering project. Give them the easy part, though. All they have to do is stand on the back of the seat frame to compress the cushion long enough for you to pull the cover into place.

This makes it a lot easier to stretch the material for a nice, tight fit.

It's smart to do one final check before you reinstall your seat. Make sure your seams line up at the back-rest and along all the edges. Other-wise, the crookedness will drive you crazy later. All you have to do now is to reinstall your seats onto their rail-ings. Smearing a thin layer of grease onto the track and rails will help them slide into place smoothly.

Comfort (Up and Down)

You'll make the greatest strides toward a more comfortable ride by upgrading your seats. But don't stop there. Remember, the Volkswagen factory was nothing if not efficient and economical. That means there were no bells, no whistles, and very little in the way of comfort-boosting touches.

Sound Deadening

If you invest in some custom upgrades, you may want to turn your attention to the sound of silence. Stock Beetles come with very little in the way of sound deadening. With-out some modification, not only will you hear lots of engine and road noise but you'll also feel the heat coming up from the asphalt.

Sound deadening has a layer of poly butyl (a synthetic rubber com-pound) backed by a self-sticking foil surface. There are many manufactur-ers, and most offer a range of thick-nesses. There is a spray-on option, but it's extremely messy to work with, so you may get much better results with the peel-and-stick type. Whatever you choose, it can be purchased from your favorite Volkswagen parts house or most local auto parts stores.

Assuming that you've removed the entire interior of your Beetle, cut the material to shape, peel the backing off, and press the sound deadener in place. Be careful, though, and wear some thick work gloves. The edges are sharp aluminum that can easily cut you. Work on one panel at a time, peel, stick, flatten with a rolling tool, and then trim the edges. Keep any decent-sized scraps to use on other projects or to fill any spots that you cut too small.

Headliner

Again, the Volkswagen factory was not especially generous in its use of padding. That frugal choice made sense in cars that were built for the masses. However, if you'd like a quieter, cozier, more luxurious ride, add more of the soft stuff before replacing your headliner.

We recommend using jute or felt. You may have some material left over after recovering your seats. If not, it can be purchased from the usual sources: your favorite VW parts house, a local auto parts shop, or even online.

The VW factory's idea of sound deadening was kind of a joke. With modern sound deadeners, you'll enjoy a quieter ride. Plus, when you shut the door, you'll get that satisfying thud *sound.*

 Tools Required

Gather the following tools and equipment:
- Sharp scissors
- Contact cement
- Mason jar (so you don't dip your brush directly into the contact cement)
- Paint brush

If you're doing a pan-off restoration, one of the first steps is adding sound deadening to your pans. This way you have easy access while you work, rather than having to perform automotive yoga.

It can be overkill, but when doing jute padding, we like to do the roof as well. It seems to help with road noise and temperature control.

When you work with your headliner and padding, be sure to work in a well-ventilated area. You'll be using contact cement, and the fumes will either give you a psychedelic trip or a bad headache. You may want to enlist the help of your most patient friend so that one of you can hold the felt in place while the other cuts it to fit.

Headliner and Padding Installation

1 *When doing a headliner, do the B-pillar first. It's as simple as inserting the windlace into the tabs along the B-pillar.*

2 *Headliners require stretching, typically over the course of a couple of days. It's about heating, stretching, and adjusting alligator clips until the wrinkles disappear. We typically stretch three times.*

3 *The second stretch is in process. Always work front to back to get the middle first, then side to side. Stock up on alligator clips.*

4 *In the third stretch, all of the wrinkles should be gone from the headliner. You're almost ready to glue it in place.*

Headliner and Padding Installation *continued*

5 *Inspect your headliner for bow straightness before you start gluing. It should look like the final state of your headliner, except for the alligator clips.*

6 *It's almost time to set the windows now that your headliner is fully stretched and glued. A rubber glass seal will help keep everything in place.*

As you cut around the spots where your visor, rearview mirror, seat belt anchor points, and courtesy handle go, make your life easier by installing the screws into their holes now. You'll be able to feel them through the felt, cut little holes, and install the screws for good when you're ready.

Your eyes should be on the road as you drive, not the inside of your Beetle's roof, but that doesn't mean your headliner doesn't deserve a little beautification. You can use just about any material known to humankind. We've seen tweed, perforated vinyl, faux leather, microfiber, and velour. They're all available from VW parts houses. But you could use any material that tickles your fancy if you want to make it your own. Most owners choose a headliner that coordinates with or matches the rest of their interior. Perforated vinyl will provide a stock look.

Right out of the box, you'll notice your new headliner is creased and wrinkly. The safest way to get it smooth is to lay it flat for a few days before you try to install it. The headliner comes precut into pieces: two go in the back, one for each side window, one for each B-pillar, a small piece that goes underneath the rear window, and one main piece. You'll also receive bows to help the headliner keep its shape. They'll go into channels sewn into the fabric. The trick is matching the bows to the channels.

Carpet

We looked up. Now, it's time to look down at your feet. While nobody will ever accuse a stock Beetle's carpet of being a treat for the feet, that just means there's plenty of room for improvement. The choices are nearly endless among the different manufacturers and materials. We've even seen fake fur and bamboo flooring! Cocoa mats can also fit the bill for certain looks.

The top of the line is German square-weave carpet. It's expensive, of course. But it's nice, dense, woolly, and will last a lifetime. Plus, it's easy to clean and the carpet kits typically fit better when you install them than stock carpet.

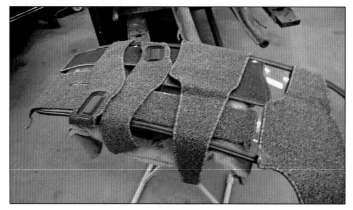

When unboxing your carpet kit, inspect it to make sure all the pieces are present. Get a kit with the carpet edges bound so that you don't end up with frayed edges.

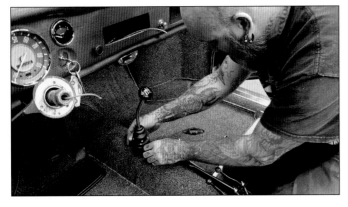

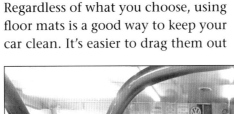

Whether you have a stock shifter or a performance shifter, you might have to do a little trimming on your tunnel carpet to get it all to function correctly. A quality kit will probably fit right out of the box.

and vacuum them than to vacuum your whole vehicle.

Comfort (Side to Side)

We've looked up. We've looked down. With your headliner and carpet looking sharp, now it's time to look side to side. Your door cards, armrests, door handles, and window cranks have room for improvement too. While the stock parts might have held up well over the decades, they might also now be cracked, discolored, and rough looking.

There's more carpet in your Bug than you might imagine. Of course, there's the whole floor. But you'll also find carpet on the backside of your back seat and under your rear window.

Floor Mats

This may be the single easiest customization that you can make to your Beetle. While you will need to make sure that the set you choose fits your Bug, there's a wide selection available. Plus, you can make your own if you feel particularly industrious.

It's probably best to choose mats that go with the rest of your interior, unless you're trying to make a statement with odd mats. What statement that might be is up for discussion. Regardless of what you choose, using floor mats is a good way to keep your car clean. It's easier to drag them out

Cocoa mats are pretty durable. They make a great choice for convertibles or Things. It's generally a natural fiber, available from several online suppliers.

Stock door panels are a good way to freshen up your interior. New armrests and door-latch escutcheons complete the look.

The original Volkswagen door cards were made of a cardboard-like fiber. They are susceptible to moisture. This is what moisture damage looks like from leaky windows.

Whether it's pinstripe or paint, you can color-match the accents of your car's interior to give a pop of color. It's the little touches that make a big impact.

Door Cards

Your best bet for customizing your door cards is to match the interior style and color. You can also choose an accent color that will highlight other colors you've used in your design. You're not limited to fabric, though. Some manufacturers make bamboo door cards. A trip to a car show will give you other ideas from license plates to Mexican blankets and denim. Find your new set at your favorite auto interior supplier or make them yourself.

Even with off-the-shelf door cards, a slight custom look is easy to achieve. Bought this way, they are not particularly expensive.

Sometimes the most subtle of touches can have a big impact. Color-matched piping on the armrest completes the look on this 1959 Beetle ragtop.

Armrests

If you don't want to go with stock, you have some options. You could cover your armrests with fabric or just remove them entirely. Some Beetle owners get pretty creative—especially those with steampunk design sensibilities. They'll swap the stock armrest out to go with a length of pipe or various other unique design options. You can buy new from a Volkswagen parts house.

Door Handles and Window Cranks

Even with a part as seemingly overlooked as interior door handles, there's room for customization. Some Beetle owners dechrome and paint theirs. Others get them powder coated. Some make their own. You can find a wide selection of styles right off the shelves of your favorite Volkswagen parts house.

Shifter

For a simple stick, there sure are a lot of options to consider. You can choose a shifter that fits your body and makes driving more comfortable.

EMPI shifters are a slight upgrade from the factory equipment. They're inexpensive, but as with this one, you'll enjoy a quicker shift with a shorter "throw." The reverse lockout is nice as well.

This shifter is made by Vintage Speed. Stylistically, it looks more like a stock shifter. However, it works better and you'll have much smoother shifting.

Gene Burg shifters have been around for a long time. They're always a good, reliable choice. Originals are a bit pricey.

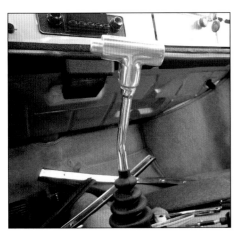

Here's another version of an EMPI shifter. This is a T-handle. The reverse lockout button is by the thumb. Some drivers find them more comfortable for shifting.

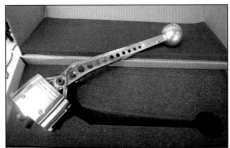

Here's a shifter from CoolRydes Customs, called the CRC Shifter. It's pricey, but it's also one of the best on the market. It's hand-built in the United States.

You can always add a touch of class with a banjo steering wheel. This one features an aftermarket zodiac horn button, which is one of many styles available.

From short throws to extra-long, your shifter should be easy to reach and even easier to use.

You can also customize the shift knob. There's one for every style, theme, and taste. We've seen golf balls, billiard balls, spent grenades, T-bars, and skulls, but really, that just scratches the surface of choices. There is also 3-D printing, which will open this field even further as Beetle owners custom-print shift knobs to match their unique preferences.

Steering Wheel

There's no other auto part you'll touch more than your steering wheel. The classic 356 banjo style is popular. Reminiscent of older Porsches, it's a classy little upgrade. Other options include smaller steering wheels as well as those covered in vinyl or leather, plus wheels coated in Bakelite or even made from wood. As vast as the option range is, many Beetle owners would agree that the originals are often cooler-looking than their aftermarket counterparts.

Theoretically, any steering wheel from any make and model could work in your Beetle. You'd just need to make sure you won't have alignment issues if you make a swap. Check that the steering spline shaft lines up with the steering wheel hub. There are adapters on the market too.

Lighting

Custom interior lighting and gauges are little touches that you'll enjoy showing off. These modifications can be as easy as unscrewing the stock piece and replacing it with something new.

Cabin Lights

What came standard is fine, but you can repurpose the wiring circuit to create much cooler looks. It'll take some wiring practice, but if you can follow a wiring diagram, you can do this yourself.

Some popular options include adding light-emitting diode (LED) light strips under the seat, under the dashboard, and even in the rear footwells. These lights will light up when you open the door. Options are limited only to the colors that come in the kit you buy.

Try not to get carried away with too many LEDs because it will overpower the other design elements in the car. Stealth is style, but do what pleases you.

The availability of 12-volt LED lighting has grown. The sizes have gotten smaller, and they're easy to hide. You can create custom lighting on a budget by using them.

A good place to hide LED lights is underneath the seat rails. Make sure the wires aren't near any moving parts or pinch points.

Gauges

You can get custom gauge face inserts created for your Beetle online. This opens virtually endless possibilities. Some companies sell ready-made gauge faces you can install quickly; others sell aftermarket gauges that may require significant modifications to your dashboard to make them fit.

If you're giving your Beetle a fresh paint job, handle those modifications during the paint and polish phase of your project. Porsche gauges are rather popular these days. But above all, remember that you have no computer on board. Most modern gauges are computer-run rather than mechanical, so be sure to get a set you can actually use.

There is a wide variety of aftermarket gauges available. You may have to do a little cutting and welding, but with some imagination, you can make a custom gauge cluster.

Another subtle touch you can add is a custom inlay in your speedometer. This one is a vinyl cutout decal. Some rebuilders of speedometers will use your custom artwork during restoration.

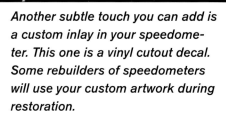

Sometimes stock should be left alone. It's timeless and classic. You can get your factory gauges rebuilt to look and work like new again.

BODY AND PAINT

A 1965 Beetle freshly restored and looking cleaner than the day it rolled out of the dealer's showroom has a custom Bahama Blue color that makes this Bug pop.

Homeowners who want to customize their living space know that the simplest and fastest way to make a dramatic change is to buy paint and some brushes, rollers, and drop cloths, and then to spend a weekend on a ladder. It would make logical sense to assume that painting your Beetle would be an equally simple and quick project.

Dub-loving friends, do not fall for that faulty line of reasoning! Unless your plan involves a rattle can (our affectionate name for spray paint), painting your Bug is a significant undertaking. Add in any bodywork you want to do to modify or restore your car, and you are in for a bigger project than you can imagine.

That's not to dissuade you from taking it on. In many cases, it makes a lot of sense to do some paint and bodywork on your ride as you customize it. After all, if it has rust (visible or not) that you allow to take over, there's not much point in swapping

While the original paint job has faded over time and the Bug could do with a good paint correction, it still looks good. This 1958 could definitely use some freshening up.

Some cars weather better than others when exposed to the elements. This 1952 Zwitter was stored under a tarp and was lived in by feral cats.

When doing a restoration, don't be shocked to find acorns and other items animals have stashed away for safekeeping. This is completely normal.

of daring-do with a welder and other metal-shaping tools, you can change the very silhouette of your car.

The number of paint color options that the Volkswagen factory offered in any particular year of production could usually be counted on one hand. For stock Beetle enthusiasts, the best plan is to repaint it the color in which it entered the world. But for those who want a custom look, there are literally thousands of paint colors from which to choose. Nothing makes a bigger immediate impact than a beautiful paint job.

Old-Fashioned Body Modifications

In a time when most automotive manufacturers shy away from the heavy metal of decades past, today's cars are lighter than ever. On average, about 30 percent of a modern vehicle consists of plastic, fiberglass, and composite material. Some say that there are environmental reasons for the shift away from metal. However, in the "old days," car bodies were made of steel.

The downside of steel is corrosion, the unyielding, unrelenting cancer that eats our Dubs out from under us. Rust cannot be stopped. However, it can be slowed significantly. The upside of steel is that this metal can be shaped.

With some practice and extraordinary levels of patience, you can become a "panel beater" or "metal shaper." For someone with these skill sets, there is no real limit on the range of modifications that you can make to your car's body.

These are not skills taught in high schools or even trade schools these days. Autobody training programs focus more on teaching students how

your stock rims for something with more personality.

If your Beetle needs restoration work done first, you should check out CarTech's *How to Restore Your Volkswagen Beetle* for solid guidance, whether you do it yourself or take your car to a

shop. There's no point in icing a cake that's on the verge of collapsing.

Assuming that your Beetle's body is in good shape, let's talk about how to make some of the most dramatic changes possible. Depending on your vision for your Bug and your sense

In most cases, project cars that have been stored outside have some of the disassembly work already done for you. In this case, the Bug came with nothing but metal inside.

For steel cars with six decades or so of experience on them, rust is a certainty. The question is not whether it's rusty but how much rust is there.

The first tool of the trade is patience. You have to understand how metal moves. Hammers, dollies, and shrinking discs come after understanding.

to change panels, use paintless dent removal equipment, and perform Small and Medium Area Repair Technique (SMART) repairs. Metalworkers now are mostly involved in fabrication for construction purposes.

However, there was a time when a hammer and dolly meant something. These artisans understood the fluid nature of steel. They knew how to coax metal into any shape and form they wished, limited only by their physical endurance and patience.

A few minutes with a shrinking disc and a cold, wet rag will start to realign the sheet metal back into its original pressing location. It wants to get back in shape.

A few hours of shrinking, stretching, bumping, and hammering steel will save you from having to use much filler. Less filler is better.

It's not easy work. You will ache in places you never dreamed possible. However, there may not be any work that is more satisfying than bending and shaping steel to conform to the vision you have in your head for your car.

Expert-Level Metal Shaping

The Airkooled Kustoms team has some rather accomplished rough and finished metal craftsmen. But we call on metal-shaping specialist Kerry Pinkerton when clients want metal modifications that call for a level of expertise beyond our own. We joke that Kerry's metal-shaping skills make us look like a bunch of cavemen beating a tin can with rocks. To know, learn from, and occasionally call upon an artisan with such master-level skills is rare.

We brought Kerry in to work on a project where the client wanted his hood to look like that of a Porsche

There will be a lot of cutting, grinding, and welding needed to get back to good bones. Keep a fire extinguisher handy.

356. The restoration project car was a Karmann Ghia, not a Beetle. However, something similar could be done on a Beetle or any other vintage vehicle.

Metal shaping involves changing the surface area of a panel, which changes its three-dimensional shape. There are only four things that you can do to metal. You can stretch it, which increases the surface area. You can shrink it, which decreases the surface area. You can also bend or fold it, but that is metal forming, not metal shaping because the surface area does not change noticeably. Finally, you can cut and weld (or glue, rivet, etc.) to create a shape. This is fabrication; it's not metal shaping. A metal shaper uses all these techniques, but the actual shaping is only stretching and shrinking.

Did You Know?

Many people are surprised to hear that metal flows under pressure, exactly like modeling clay would. The metal enters a plastic state and literally flows in the path of least resistance. The trick is knowing how and why to apply pressure to have the metal end up in the desired shape. This takes experience.

Stretching is easy. There are many ways to do it. Basically, the metal is thinned in the desired area by hitting it with a hammer, rolling it through a wheeling machine (English wheel), putting it in a press to squeeze it, or using any number of other manual or power machines and techniques. As the metal is thinned, the surface area increases and the panel becomes deeper.

The Type 1 Karmann Ghia is based on the VW Beetle chassis. It shares at least half of its components with its more popular cousin.

If you feel yourself getting frustrated while you're shaping metal, walk away and come back later. This is about finesse, not force.

A metal finish is always preferable to sculpting filler. With a few hours of work, you can save time on the back end of the process in the body shop.

Think of a bowl. If you start with a round disc of metal and stretch just the center, the surface area will increase and the disc will start to take a bowl shape. How deep the bowl is depends on how far you stretch it. The more you continue to stretch, the deeper the bowl will become. The potential depth of the bowl is limited by how much metal with which you

have to work. Ultimately, you could stretch the metal so thin that it will tear.

The metal will also become work-hardened as it is worked. This makes the metal hard and difficult to work. The way to relieve the work-hardening stresses is to planish it. Planishing involves hammering lightly many times, usually over a

dolly. Planishing can also be done with a mechanical or pneumatic planishing hammer or an English wheel. Once the metal has been planished, it can be worked again.

The other side of metal shaping involves shrinking. Shrinking is much more difficult than stretching. That's because the metal has to be moved in such a way that when it

While a pneumatic hammer or planisher is not strictly required to do this type of work, it does make it easier to move metal faster. You can do it with a hammer and dolly; it'll just take longer.

Shrinkers and stretchers are invaluable tools in the metal shop. They help create complex curves fairly easily.

goes into the plastic stage and flows in the path of least resistance, it flows *into* itself and gets thicker.

Shrinking can be done with hand tools, but it is typically done with mechanical shrinkers, both manual and powered. Shrinking deep into a panel requires considerable force, and the tools that do this can be quite expensive—into the thousands and tens of thousands of dollars. Some of the machines that do this are called power hammers, reciprocating machines, such as Pullmax and Trumph, and Eckold KraftFormers.

Typically, shrinking involves gripping the metal with mechanical jaws and pushing those jaws together. Other techniques flow the metal into itself by using special dies called thumbnail dies.

Back to our bowl example, if you shrink the edges of the disk, the surface area decreases, and the shape of the bowl decreases. Most bowl shapes end up with stretched centers (thinner) and shrunk edges (thicker). Metal shaping is a recursive process. You stretch, shrink, smooth, test fit, and repeat until you achieve the desired shape.

In the universe, there are only three basic shapes: compound curves (three-dimensional bowls), simple rolls (two-dimensional bends), and flat. Everything is a combination of one or more of these shapes. Flat shapes can be cut from the sheet as purchased. Simple rolls can be bent in a sheet-metal brake, pushed around a pipe, or even bent over your knee. Compound curves are made by stretching, shrinking, and smoothing.

Metal shapers often combine these three shapes to complete the job required. The more competent the shaper, the better a complex panel can be made in one piece. But that may not be the most efficient use of time and material. A good weld can save lots of time and money.

Example: Hood Modification

On this hood, Kerry put two Porsche vents where the original stamped vents were. Then, he shaped the panels to replace the areas between and on either side of the new vents.

The hood centerline was carefully determined and marked. All subsequent modifications were made relative to this reference line. Measure carefully so that you don't face challenges when it's time to reassemble the car.

The original hood also has a character line that has to be removed and smoothed. The Porsche vents will need modification to line up well with the hood's curve. Pay close attention to how well the lines and curves flow for the best results.

The curve of the Porsche's engine lid does not match the curve of the Volkswagen's hood, so some modification to the vents will be necessary. In addition, a good bit of the inner structure has to be removed for access

When doing custom metalwork, it's important to figure out what you want first. Lay it out and line it up before making any cuts.

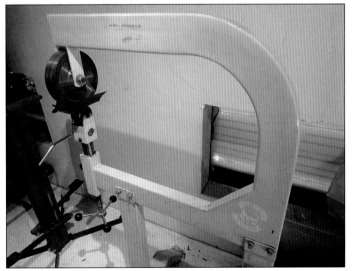

An English wheel is vital for doing custom sheet metal. It can create compound curves front to back and right to left.

to both sides of the hood. A new drip panel will be shaped to fit below the vents to catch rainwater and direct it away from the engine compartment. After all, we can't be having water spots on that pretty engine, can we?

Once the inner structure was cut away, Kerry determined that the character line could just be reversed and smoothed. To do this, he used his English wheel. Light pressure was used to avoid significant stretching.

After a few passes, the character line was gone and the profile was smooth. If the profile had not flowed smoothly, some shrinking would have been required. There are several ways to do an interior panel shrink, but a shrinking disk mounted on a large body grinder would probably have been the tool of choice.

Patch panels to fill the old stamped vents were rolled on the English wheel to produce the cor-

rect crown. The masking tape on the edges can be felt when wheeling and keeps the metal from being stretched on the edge.

The non-stretched edge is what constrains the stretched inner portion and allows the crown to develop. If the panel had been stretched all over, it would still be flat but just bigger. If you've ever made a pie crust or watched someone making one, this process is much the same.

We wanted to remove this crease in the body to clean up the lines. It came creased from the factory. The English wheel will smooth it out.

Post-English wheel, this decklid is ready for hammer, dolly, and shrinking disc work. Each process is a step toward completion.

Now, we're using the English wheel to take flat steel and match the curves for the patch panels in the decklid. It's a slight and subtle complex curve.

We're smoothing out this body line. It's almost ready for hammer and dolly work. By smoothing it first and matching the factory curves, you can clean up the body lines.

Time to get serious and cut some metal. A rough cut was made for the new vent opening and to remove the old vents. Always use personal safety equipment. Nothing hurts like getting metal bits in your eye.

A piece of 19-gauge (18 would have worked) steel was bent to a 1/2 x 3/4–inch angle. This was then stretched in four corners so the new vent fit inside it with no visible gap.

Although a cheap Lancaster-type shrinker/stretcher could have been used, that type of tool uses file-like teeth. It can easily put stress risers in the metal, which will lead to cracking. Kerry used his large shop-built kick shrinker and stretcher with Marchant-style tooling.

This tooling uses stippled dies and is much easier on the metal. The stretcher is identical, but its tooling pulls away from each other, thinning it. Too much pressure can cause the metal to tear. Slow and steady is the key, along with trial fits—a lot of trial fits.

After all four corners of the top edge were stretched to fit evenly around the new vents, it was welded together into a rectangle. The vertical edge needed to be shrunk in order to fit the downward curve of the hood. It is a similar process. As the metal is shrunk, it curves down.

Again, slow and steady work

Using the English wheel, we're creating a patch panel with a double compound curve. Note that we are using a piece of steel that is larger than required. It will be trimmed to fit later.

We've measured and cut out the new opening for the custom grilles. We also cleaned the paint off the steel of the decklid so we can weld the new bracket and patch panels in.

We're test fitting the insert for the new grilles before scribing and welding them in. Make any adjustments needed before welding.

We made the replacement panel a little larger than the hole required. Next, we'll scribe it to fit the opening before cutting. We got a nice tight fit.

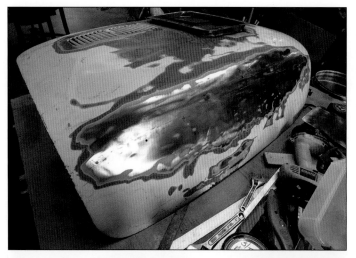

You can see here the overall look we're going for with the twin 356 grilles instead of the factory air intake. We've smoothed the body lines considerably.

We used a 356 grille as a template to create the opening we'll insert in the decklid. Remember to leave a little room for the seals that go between the frame and the grille.

One last lineup and clamping in place before welding. We've left the filler panel out to do this part of the process so we can get clean lines.

With the grilles, we needed to add a rain tray that looks like it could have come from the factory. We also wanted to make it removable for cleaning, so we included Zeus fasteners.

With a bit of shrinking and stretching, hard radius curves are achievable. This almost looks like it came from the factory this way.

along with many trial fits is the key. If Kerry went too far, the stretcher could have been used to correct the result. By the time the metal shaping was complete, you would never know that this hood came from the factory looking any different.

Once everything fit correctly, it was time to scribe and cut. Accuracy is very important. Metal shrinks during welding, and you don't want to deal with large gaps that require lots of filler. That causes warpage that has to be tediously corrected.

The many drilled holes in the hood were also TIG welded shut, ground, and planished to stretch the hood back into the correct profile. Once the metal was cut, the pieces were welded with a TIG. A MIG welder could have been used but is more difficult to finish because of the heat that is introduced into the panel.

The new hood needed a new drip shield below the vents. Although this could have been done many ways, Kerry used shrinking dies to turn the

After all the cutting, welding, hammering, and grinding is done, protect your work by applying three coats of epoxy primer. This will help slow corrosion.

Before the final sealer, do one more test fit for the grilles. This is an important step because you don't want to have to make adjustments on a freshly painted surface.

edges of a baking sheet–like panel. This allowed the Airkooled Kustoms team to reinstall the internal structure and incorporate the new drip pan.

While doing this type of radical metal shaping well is probably out of reach for most hobbyists, you may find that you have a knack for basic metalwork. The only way to find out is to try it on a less ambitious project. However, we wanted to show you what's possible if you can find a skilled craftsman.

Just Add Color

Assuming that you're working with a Beetle that is sound and smooth, the next modification you might want to make is the paint. There may be no more impactful customizing touch that you can add to make a Bug *your* Bug. The options boil down to the following: wraps, patina, candy patina, or custom paint.

Wraps

It almost pains us to include wraps in the list of options. They are seen as a shortcut, and because we steer clear of shortcuts as a rule, the shop doesn't do them. Since we specialize in full restorations, we take all panels down to bare steel, restore them, and then spend an ungodly number of hours painting and polishing to make Beetles shiny and straight.

Wraps are not quite the same. In fact, aside from disagreeing with them on principle, there is an objective concern with using them. While a wrap will protect the exterior side of a panel from rust, the underside is another matter. With a wrap in place,

you might not notice that your baby is rusting right before your eyes.

Now, wraps have come a long way over the years, but even with the improvements that manufacturers have made, wraps are still wraps. For most Beetle owners, wraps are probably not a suitable choice. There is an exception. For the drag racer subset of Bug drivers, wraps make a lot of sense.

In drag racing, it's all about decreasing a car's weight while getting the most power possible from the engine. Paint weighs more than a wrap. It's also possible to use a ceramic coating, specially formulated for vinyl wraps, to add a sacrificial layer that protects the wrap.

Drag strips are wildly different settings from where most Beetle owners would take their cars. Having the ability to withstand the impact of debris flying at high velocity is a perk that wraps can deliver better than most paint jobs. There's also an endless range of design possibilities, since wraps can be custom made.

Patina

Given enough time and exposure to the elements, every Beetle

Patina comes in all shapes and forms. Some are natural, and some are recreated. Can you tell which is which here?

becomes a patina monster. That's our affectionate name for vehicles we see that are so rusty that they defy the laws of nature to hold themselves in a solid state. Patina can be absolutely gorgeous or, honestly, hideous. It's all a matter of personal opinion and preference.

Patina is a look that shows off the ravages of time and highlights the history of a vehicle that was decades in the making. Assuming that your Beetle's finish pleases your eyes, your rust is not causing any structural concerns, and you're up to date on your tetanus vaccination, this may be a great choice for you.

With a patina ride, you are virtually guaranteed to have a Bug like nobody else's. You won't have to worry about road debris, weather-related damage, or theft. Actually, as popular as patina is in some circles, theft may be a possibility, so make sure to protect your baby no matter how rusty it is.

Just enjoy your patina Beetle as is. Over time, nature will continue to work on your paint finish, completing the patina look. At any point, if you decide it's time to strip your Beetle and repaint, you always have that option. Just keep an eye out for rust that's getting out of hand.

While it's possible to restore nearly any Bug in any condition, the price tag for doing so can reach astronomical heights. If you let the rust go too far, you may reach a point where nothing much is salvageable, especially if you don't have oodles of cash to spend on replacing panels and paying for metalwork.

Candy Patina

If you love your patina finish, there's a way you can preserve it from being ravaged by rust. By add-

Another option is a candy patina. This involves prepping the existing paint before applying clear coat layers.

ing a protective clear finish coat on top of the patina, you'll get a bit of shine. But more importantly, you can help slow the progress of corrosion, at least from the outside of the panels. The underside of the metal will still actively rust, and eventually you'll need to find another solution.

If you want to buy yourself some time before repainting or if you love how nature has had its way with your Bug, a candy patina finish may be just what you want. If your patina is uneven, you can even create a sort of faux patina to spread the look over the entire car. You can accomplish that look by getting creative with sandpaper and maybe even some carefully chosen automotive paints that mimic and complement the colors already in the finish.

CarTech has a book titled *Patina: How to Paint and Preserve*, which is an absolute must-have item if creating

CarTech's Patina: How to Paint and Preserve *covers everything from creating faux patina to preserving existing patina. It also covers how to recover from mistakes and the tools that are needed to create your masterpiece.*

or preserving your patina is the route that you select.

Harlequin

You can also go with multiple colors, and as long as you choose the

The Harley Quinn is exactly what you would image, per this rendering by Airkooled Kustoms.

hues well, you'll get a really nice and unique look. For the truly undecided, there's always a Harlequin look, which is traditionally done with bright shades of red, green, yellow, and blue.

While you would be forgiven for assuming that these cars were built from whatever parts the owner happened to salvage, you'd be wrong. Volkswagen shoulders the blame (or credit, depending on your perspective) for this unusual design choice. The bold design choice rolled off the Volkswagen factory line in the form of the 1996 Golf, which many detractors nicknamed the "weird-mobile" for good reason.

Volkswagen has long been known for its dry wit–filled ads. Perhaps the Harlequin was a practical joke? No matter, those who love them really love them. The color scheme spread from Golfs to Beetles, and you may see one at a car show (unless you avert your eyes, that is).

Legend has it that an Atlanta, Georgia, VW dealership had a few of these Golfs on its lot during the 1996 Olympics. Shockingly, these cars didn't sell, no matter how hard the dealership tried to make them disappear. The legend says that late one

night, the dealership owner sent the four back to the service area. There, the technician team disassembled all of the bodies and sorted the panels by color. By the time morning came, the lot mysteriously had four new Golfs to sell: one red, one green, one yellow, and one blue.

Shiny Paint

This is our specialty, and we get a bit obsessed. In fact, our clients typically only pay for a small portion of the labor that we put into our paint finishes. It's not that we're especially generous; it's more that it pains us to let a Dub go out with flaws. So, there have been multiple instances

of our painters and polishers spending untold hours fixing flaws that no sane human would even notice.

In choosing new paint colors, every hue imaginable is available. Plus, by adding white, blue, silver, or gold metallic flake into the mix, you can create looks that range from a subtle slimmer to bass boat levels of glitz.

When it comes to straight, shiny, glass-like paint, the bulk of your blood, sweat, and tears has nothing to do with the actual paint. It's all about the surface preparation. The smoother your panels, the better you'll be able to lay the paint down.

You can't slather your Beetle

Some paint corrections can take hundreds of hours to perform. While you can spend that much time to achieve a mirror-like gloss, be careful not to take your paint off.

with Bondo and expect it to look gloriously smooth. There simply is no substitute for doing the bodywork right. It will take longer and demand more work than you can imagine. That's why many vintage car owners entrust their projects to professionals.

Working just on weekends, it could easily take years to prepare the body properly for paint, if you're after a near-perfect look. Of course, the goal for most Volkswagen owners is to get maximum enjoyment from their rides. Perfect paint is lovely, but optional.

Major Custom Paint Upgrades

The range of premade and custom-formulated paint colors is virtually endless. Yet, for some Beetle owners, even a trio of specially chosen colors isn't quite enough to set their ride apart from all others. Just as in home decor, there are no rules about what can be done with paint.

From what goes into the paint to how it's applied to the car's body, these paint modifications add one

This airbrushed piece was done by Michael Swann. To personalize your Beetle to an extreme, you could get any image that you like painted as an inlay. Just add clear coat on top for protection.

more unique layer to any ride. As always, the only limitation is your imagination. Whether you wield the paint gun yourself or seek expert help, you can recreate the vision in your imagination on the panels of your Beetle.

Inlays

If you likened paint inlays to getting a tattoo, you wouldn't be far off. You could go with a geometric design or line art. You could do to your Beetle what lowriders do to big, long sedans every day: add some

This is a two-stage paint job. We painted the base color, applied a vinyl sticker, then painted the bling color on top. Finally, we removed the vinyl sticker and applied the clear.

Don't be afraid of bright colors as a trim accent. Our Jolly Rancher green is a custom mix that looks good on this Beetle.

With a slight gold metallic mica in the base green, you'll see a subtle color shift in the sunlight. This adds character and depth to your paint job.

bling, draw some lines, and make it pop. However, in this case, the owner wanted to tip his hat to some favorite characters from another of his passions: comics and anime.

The owner of this 1965 Type 1 Beetle reached the point in his life and career when it was time to get the car he really wanted. Realizing that he could either drop the same amount of money on a brand-new car that would blend in with every other car on the road or go for a brand-new old classic Dub, he went with character. His Beetle boasts a black chrome paint job highlighted with Jolly Rancher metallic green and a custom mural on the decklid that was imagined and designed by the client.

We accomplished this look by first painting his Beetle with a blingy-black chrome base. Then, we added the accent color, a sort of seafoam green, to the running boards and a few other components. But then came the magic touch of an airbrush artist. The image began with a sketch, using original images of the characters for reference. Then, came layer upon layer of lines and fill, until the final result matched what the client envisioned.

Additives: Metal Flake and Pearl Paint

"Wait until you see it outside in the sunlight."

That's often the response you'll receive if you compliment Spook on a newly finished paint job at the shop. Indoors, under LED lights, the paint looks slick, glossy, and mirror-like. You could read in the reflection; it's that shiny. But, if you take a panel outdoors on a sunny day, you'll reach an entirely new level of appreciation for the magic of paint.

In some cases, you'll find yourself questioning your initial assessment of what color the paint is. Black shifts to blue. Green shifts to brown or gold. The deepest red takes on a silver shimmer. It all depends on what went into the paint. You can add different colors and sizes of metallic particles, or flake, into the mix. These particles reflect light and add a spectacular look.

Likewise, you can choose a pearlescent paint. Unlike metallic flake, pearlescent paint contains ceramic particles, also called mica, that both reflect and refract the light. Where a metallic flake makes your Beetle shine, a pearl makes it glow.

Despite the beautiful look that either of these paint modifications can give your ride, there are a few warnings to note. First, excellent automotive paint is expensive. It's not uncommon for a single gallon of paint to cost hundreds or even nearly a thousand dollars. Add flake or mica, and the price goes up from there.

Second, specialty paint is all fun and games until someone's Beetle gets dinged. Repair work is even trickier when you have to match custom paint. Even if you were to have easy access to the original paint formulation, you'll find yourself painting much more surface area than just where the damage occurred. Still, this kind of paint modification turns heads and makes any vehicle stand out.

Marbelizing

Years ago, the faux-paint trend became hot in home decor. Ragging, rolling, stippling, and other home improvement staples found their way into homes everywhere. Some of those techniques also work in automotive paint. It can add a little extra interest to what would otherwise be a solid-colored component.

We used a marbelizing technique to add some interest to the dashboard of a 1961 Double Cab. After the base coat went down, we used plastic wrap to create the look. Simply paint the surface with the accent color. Before that coat dries, scrunch some plastic wrap up slightly, then daub at the paint to pull it off the surface.

You should experiment with different thicknesses of paint and using different objects to remove the paint (for instance, more or less tightly scrunched plastic, natural sponges, or rags). You could even reverse the process and add your secondary paint using a non-brush object. Practice until you achieve the look you imagined.

You can add a one-of-a-kind look with marbelizing techniques. Just be sure to use two contrasting colors to make your artwork visible.

Pinstriping

You might think of pinstriping as intentional, self-inflicted graffiti. It's usually a subtle effect, just enough to make your ride stand out from all others. If you get the chance to watch a pinstripe artist at work, be prepared to be mesmerized. If you decide to try it yourself, be prepared for a substantial learning curve. It is not nearly as easy as it looks.

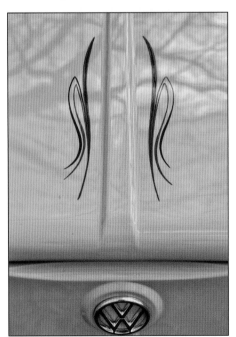

Pinstriping is a subtle artform to bring accent lines to your ride. A little bit goes a long way, and it's best to let the artist choose the colors.

You'll need to invest in the right brushes. There are multiple types, including double-lines, flats, daggers, and swords. The handle is short and the brush hairs are long. They're typically made from squirrel hair, which is interesting and confusing because it's often called camel hair.

You'll need an exceptionally steady hand, too. While there are stencils for pinstriping, the experts do it freehand. We recommend practicing on any object you can get to stay still long enough, and not just flat ones. Your Beetle has no straight, flat surfaces whatsoever; so you'll need to learn how to navigate curves. We bring in an expert when clients want pinstriping. It's best to let the artist choose the design and color, too. They know what they're doing, and if you're lucky, they'll let you watch them work.

Hydro Dipping

You may have seen baseball helmets, hockey sticks, and even hunting rifles with custom-painted patterns all over them. Sometimes it looks like camouflage, but it's not always abstract shapes and patterns. It may be hydro dipping instead. Also called water transfer, this is a fascinating process to watch.

Essentially, the hydro dipping artist prepares a water bath in a specialized tank. On the surface of the bath they'll lay a layer of hydrographic film. The film dissolves in the water, leaving a pattern floating on the water's surface. Next, they carefully dip an object into the tank, covering it neatly with the pattern. The artist then coats the object with automotive wet spray clear coat, making the pattern permanent.

Hydro dipping isn't a skill you could just pick up on a weekend, of course. It requires specialized equipment and a lot of practice. However, you may be able to find a hydro dipping business in your area. They'll have you choose your pattern and colors and bring in whatever objects you plan to hydro dip. The endless variety of paint options gives Beetle owners a dizzying range of customization choices.

This 1959 Beetle features elements that have been hydro dipped. From a distance, the mirror's casing looks like it was marbleized. Upon closer inspection, you will see the pattern includes hundreds of skulls. (Photo Courtesy Studio 810)

TRIM

While we're not huge fans of chrome, it does draw attention to details. Make sure you pay attention to the engine chapters. As they say, "Chrome won't get you home."

When it comes to bling on Beetles, it might look like the choices are all or nothing. To a chrome lover, a Bug is only complete when onlookers are blinded by the glint bouncing off all of that decorative trim. For minimalists, chrome looks so tacky they're tempted to pull it off barehanded—even if it's not their car.

Vandalistic urges aside, there may be no easier way to customize your Beetle than to modify the decorative trim. These bits of chrome can accentuate body lines and parts, and their presence or absence is a simple way to change your Bug's personality.

The first air-cooled Beetles made landfall in the United States in 1949. Onlookers at the port likely shielded their eyes as the sun reflected off all the chrome. That's because what came into the United States was the Deluxe model—"deluxe," meaning that it had trim and carpet. If that sounds a bit sparse, consider the Standard trim package that is prevalent in Europe.

The Standard model had no chrome trim, painted bumpers, and rubber floor mats. Given the economic struggles of post-war Europe, this stripped-down model offered a relatively affordable option for

Chrome won't get you home. But getting your Bug rechromed is a good way to add some bling to your ride. Just avoid using it in the engine bay.

Europeans who couldn't justify popping for the Deluxe model and its fancy trim.

Heavy chrome took off in the 1950s car culture. No one did chrome like a Studebaker, Pontiac, Meteor, or Bel Air. However, no one un-did chrome like the hot rodders who jettisoned every optional ounce of metal in pursuit of a leaner, meaner, faster ride.

Then, there are Beetle owners. We have never been the type to leave well enough alone, whether cruising or racing. Whether adding chrome or stripping it, most of these modifications are simple and affordable enough for anyone to do.

Chrome Restoration

Your choices are not limited to "chrome" and "no chrome." You can also change the look of your Beetle's chrome. Yours may be in good shape, or it may be rusty, flaking off, and discolored. The second will work well if you're driving a patina ride, but it's

Repainting chrome pieces can get you the look you're going for without adding a lot of expense. Plus, you can get whatever color you want for a custom look.

probably not quite the look that you want if you like sleek and shiny. In that case, you have some restoration options.

Painting, vinyl wrapping, hydro dipping, and rechroming are all options if your chrome has seen better days. If you decide to paint or powder coat your chrome, it'll be important to sandblast it first. That'll help you get a surface that's rough enough for paint or powder to adhere to it. Other than painting, the other options are probably best left to the pros because they require special equipment. In the case of rechroming, definitely leave it to the pros.

Working with chrome plating is dangerous. With hexavalent chromium (a known carcinogen), lead (damaging to the liver and the brain), cyanide (deadly), and cadmium (cancer plus kidney and lung disease), all that shine comes at a steep price. Chrome specialists exist who will restore the shiny bits for you. However, as it may cost them their health, you can bet it will cost you an arm and a leg too.

Now, to put your mind at ease, while the processes and chemicals involved in chrome work are highly toxic, once the work is complete, chrome is stable and safe.

If you do go with replating, you'll have a whole new appreciation for your chrome. Make sure that you take good care of it! Give it a good cleaning every couple of months using soapy water or glass cleaner. Then, give it a light coat of car wax to protect it so it lasts.

Crotch Coolers

Beetle owners are a creative lot, especially when it comes to adding more "cool" to their rides, in both

Tolerances for the VW factory were not as tight as in modern factories. Aftermarket parts manufacturers now have much better tolerances than the originals.

senses of the word. Unless you install an air-conditioning system, your ride is going to be a bit warm in the summer. Either that or you'll need to roll your windows down and mess up your hair.

However, there is another option. You can add crotch coolers. Junior-high jokes aside, let us assure you that this is indeed a real thing. Crotch coolers are the side vents that you'd typically find on the rear portion of the front quarter panel of Beetles built from 1951 to 1952.

Until 2019, you had two options if you wanted to add this quirky component to your Beetle's body. You could cut them out of a Bug that has them (and good luck finding such a donor), or you could order them online from an overseas manufacturer and hope for the best. Now, thanks to Jason Fields at Rare Air MFG in the Pacific Northwest, there's another option.

While Jason's business is relatively new, he has had a passion for fabrication and restoration since he was a young guy learning everything he could about Volkswagens. Starting in 1988, he worked in Vancouver at Autosport International (ASI), a Volkswagen shop. The shop had a wrecking yard, mechanical shop, and body shop. There, Jason received a hands-on education by disassembling every bolt, nut, and screw on their projects, and then putting them back on. He also learned his way around swap meets and car shows and learned that his meager budget for buying parts would not go very far.

A few years ago, Jason attended a swap meet where a set of crotch coolers caught his eye. He picked them up and asked for a price. The vendor wanted $550, which seemed excessive, given their condition. The springs were rusty. The hinges were sloppy. He passed on the opportunity to buy them. Not long afterward, Jason visited a friend's shop and discovered that his friend had bought them.

He borrowed the set, studied them closely, and decided that he could do better. He built dies and fabricated a new pair of reproductions. The first version came out looking beautiful but fitting poorly. They were too big. However, it was easy enough to retool and try again. The next time, they came out perfect. Throughout that process, several of Jason's friends checked on his progress. They said that when he figured out how to make them, they wanted a pair.

Of course, there were still the seals and grilles with which to contend, and Jason figured he could just order those parts from another manufacturer. He found one and tried to get a wholesale deal. The best they could do was combine shipping, which wasn't much of a savings.

When he had the opportunity to see some that a friend had ordered from that overseas manufacturer, his decision was confirmed. In addition to being fragile, the design had some flaws. The spring in the door hit the grille, causing damage.

So, Jason expanded his manufacturing process to make them as well. Seeing firsthand how important it was for the grilles to be strong, he opted to make his from stainless steel. Not only are they strong but they are also easy to polish. In fact, they should last as long as you own your car.

The craftsmanship on these crotch coolers is so good that it's not uncommon for buyers to snap up a pair long before they plan to install them. Many customers say that they are collecting parts for their "someday" build.

Crotch Cooler Installation

1 *Measure twice, cut once. Location matters, and you need to get this part into precisely the right spot of the body.*

2 *After doing your markouts, make your cuts. A very thin cutoff wheel will make this job a lot easier because it allows for much tighter cuts.*

Crotch Cooler Installation *continued*

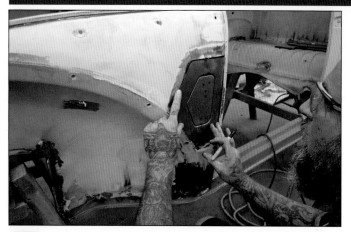

3 Test fit the panel that you're integrating into the body. You always want to cut short and make adjustments from there.

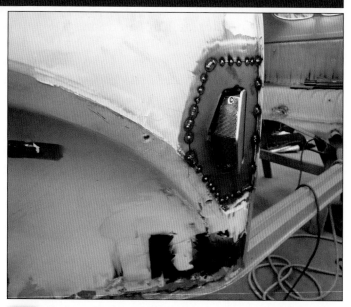

4 Tack weld the crotch coolers in place. Make sure to distribute your heat so that you don't warp the panel as you work.

5 Grind your welds down to create a nice, smooth surface for bodywork. There should be a variation of less than 1/8 inch of thickness between the two panels to keep your filler material usage to a minimum.

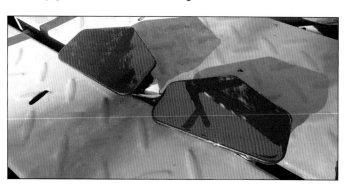

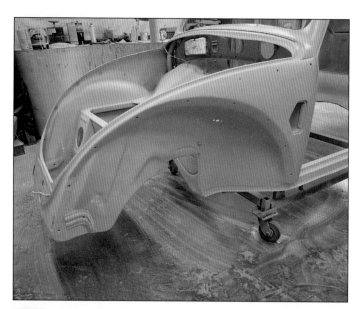

6 After doing the rough bodywork, we suggest applying a high-build primer. This will make it easy to cut and level the welded surface to match the original panel.

7 Once the bodywork is leveled, straightened, and sanded, go ahead and shoot the crotch cooler openings. Color and clear to match the body.

If you can measure, cut steel, and weld, you won't have much trouble putting crotch coolers into your Beetle's front quarter panel. Simply measure from the bottom of the front quarter panel on the driver's side. We recommend 10¾ inches from the bottom, and 1¼ inches in from the A-pillar.

Trace the inside of the inside trim plate for your primary cut on the outside. You'll be able to slide the crotch cooler interior box into that hole. There's a flange on the outside of the crotch cooler that you should trace around to show the true cut lines.

You now have your outer hole cut. Next, drill a series of pilot holes from the outside of the car, using the outer hole as a guide.

Move to the inside of the car. Line the inner trim ring up with the pilot holes and trace the inside of the trim ring to show you where to cut. There will be a little bit of cleanup work and deburring needed to make a nice, tight fit. Repeat the process to install the passenger-side crotch cooler.

Insert the crotch cooler from the outside. Weld it. After the welds are cleaned up and your bodywork is done, go to the inside and test fit your trim plate. When you like how it looks, disassemble the door and screen and paint before reassembling.

Semaphores

For most drivers, activating their car's turn signals is a humdrum experience, if they do so at all. But for those who have semaphores (also called trafficators), signaling an upcoming turn could nearly be called a public service. That's because anyone witnessing this component's little arms extending to indicate a turn is going to have to smile.

Now, note that semaphore receiver pockets will only fit on Beetles manufactured in 1964 or before. There's just not enough room on later-model posts to accommodate them.

If your Beetle is a sedan, it's relatively easy to find semaphores and their pockets to install. But if you have a convertible, you will have a tough time finding them. (By the way, did you know that every convertible Bug started out as a sedan first? If you look at the line where the chrome trim is clipped on, you will see where the factory welded a cap on top of the quarter panels and doors.)

Given the fact that "nobody" is making this aftermarket bit of kitsch and given Jason Fields's propensity to take on such fabrication challenges, it will probably not surprise you that he is also making semaphores and their pockets for convertibles. They're to be installed on the quarter panel.

With a convertible, they need to close a lot tighter, and Jason's version has a lens shaped slightly differently. He currently reproduces pockets to accept either the convertible's version, that is built for the sedan, or a deeper version.

If your Beetle already has semaphore pockets but is missing the indicators, all you need to do is install your new semaphore components and wire them to work with your turn signals. However, if you are installing semaphores in a Beetle that didn't come equipped with them from the factory, the process requires a bit of cutting and welding on your B-pillar.

Measure twice, cut once. Start on the driver's side and then repeat on the passenger's side.

The first mark to make is a centerline down the B-pillar. The second

This kit from Rare Air MFG takes the guesswork out of fitting semaphores into your Bug. Remember, semaphores were originally only in European Beetles. They were never imported that way.

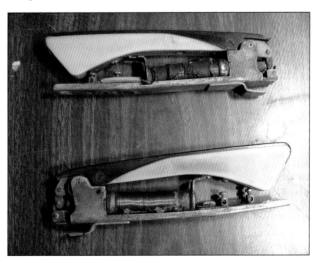

The top semaphore is not rebuilt. The bottom has undergone restoration and is ready to go. It is now a 12-volt unit.

Semaphore Installation

1 *We're hooking up the two wire connections for the semaphore. First is the positive lead going into the electromagnetic coil. Second is the ground. Make sure the connections are clean.*

2 *After putting the semaphore into the open position, slide it into the pocket. Brace yourself; this will be a tight fit.*

3 *The best practice is to slide the top in first. Then, slide the bottom in. Attach with one mounting screw into the pocket. Slide to the closed position.*

4 *After installation is complete, cycle the semaphores with the turn signal switch to make sure they function correctly. They should rise and illuminate when activated.*

is 13 inches down from the bottom edge of the drip rail. This point will be the bottom of the pocket. Then, make a horizontal line to indicate the bottom of the pocket.

After that part is square, measure 1/16 inch from the doorjamb on the B-pillar to draw a vertical line, using your pocket to get the height and width of the pocket hole. You should have a nice rectangle now. There's a flange on the outside of the sema-phore pocket that you should trace around to show the true cut lines.

Cut your pocket hole, slide the receiver into the hole, and weld it. Grind your welds and do your body-

work. You will need to wire it up by connecting it to your turn signal relay, which is connected to your indicator stalk.

The semaphore is tucked nicely away in the B-pillar on Euro-pean Bugs. It is easy to add to any Beetle using a kit as we did.

Australian Trim

You can add a little period-correct bling to your Bug by installing Aussie trim. Australian trim or Aussie flash trim is a V-shaped aftermarket decorative aluminum trim piece that goes from in front of the A-pillar to behind the C-pillar and all the way across the door.

Made by Canopy Industries in Marrickville, Sydney, Australia, the trim was available as a dealer option, depending on the dealer, but only in Australia. It was sold under the trade name of Tilli Products. Beetles were not the only car model that frequently featured this bit of bling. Vauxhall, Morris, Holden, Simca, Peugeot, and even some Fords wore it well too.

Originally, there were multiple variations of Aussie trim. Essentially, they varied in the angle of the V. Now, there's really only one style available, and it comes in stainless steel or clear-coated aluminum. You can get it from online vendors. In fact, our favorite crotch cooler and semaphore pocket manufacturer, Rare Air MFG, is gearing up to produce top-notch Aussie flash trim here in the United States.

Different manufacturers use different ways to attach the trim. The first way attaches the same way the factory's belt line trim attaches. Drill a hole that's the same size as the factory holes according to trim manufacturer's instructions.

Some manufacturers even give you a pattern. You just tape it to your car (use painter's tape!), mark your lines, and drill your holes. Also, after you've drilled your holes, you might want to take some clear nail polish or

A little bit of masking tape goes a long way. You want to protect your paint job as you fit the tabs of your Aussie trim into the holes.

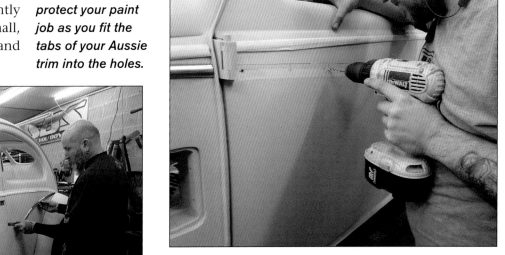

When laying your Aussie trim out, remember that these were typically hand-fit by the dealer. You'll need to make some adjustments to get yours to fit right.

When you lay out the Aussie trim, it's best to have your door panels installed first. This way you can see what the lines will look like. There were five versions of this trim originally.

two-part clear paint and go around the edge of the holes to coat any bare steel to help prevent corrosion. Install the clips into the trim. Line up the holes and clips, and snap them into place.

Some Beetle owners prefer a version that's flat on the backside. To install, use special automotive two-sided tape. Some say the profile on the flat backside version isn't quite the same as the exterior chrome trim that came standard with the Beetle. However, most casual observers won't be able to tell the difference.

Australian Trim Installation

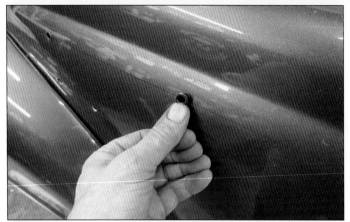

1 *Insert the rubber grommet plugs into the holes in the side of your Beetle. This will help protect against water infiltrating the inside of your car. They also help the clips stay in place.*

2 *After you've installed all the rubber grommets, go to the next step. However, first make sure that each grommet is seated properly.*

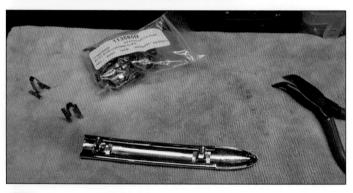

4 *Next, take the clips and slide them into your trim where it looks like an H. A small pair of needle-nose pliers is very helpful.*

3 *Up front, there are four rubber grommets that need installing for the normal trim line. There are two for the lower trim line.*

5 *Line the trim up to the A-pillar. Then, line the clips up to the grommeted holes. Slowly press the clips into the grommets.*

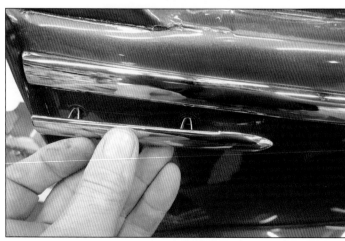

Australian Trim Installation *continued*

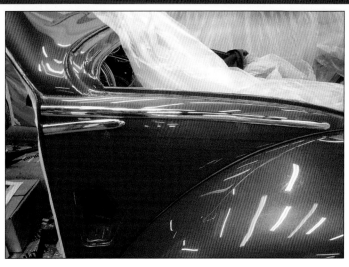

6 After everything is lined up, press the clips all the way into the grommets for a tight fit. Just use your fingers.

7 Stand back and look at your work. Make any needed fitment adjustments before setting the trim piece all the way into the grommet holes.

8 Work your trim piece in slowly and methodically. Don't do one clip all the way down. Instead, do one section a bit, then the next and the next. Then, repeat until it's all the way in.

9 It is always good to put the deluxe body line molding in first before putting the Aussie trim in. You want to be sure your alignment is correct.

10 Here the stock trim is installed and correctly adjusted. For proper alignment, this needs to be done before the Aussie or flash trim is installed.

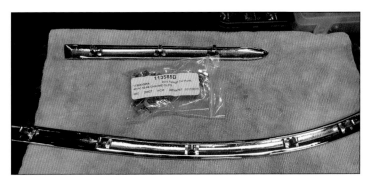

11 Next up is the Aussie trim. There are five clips that need to be installed for the down-slash trim and three clips for the diagonal trim.

12 Line up the Aussie flash trim's downward sloping section. Do this before the upward sloping trim. Align to the rear fender.

Australian Trim Installation *continued*

13 With the rear trim installed, it's time to install the small upward-sloping trim. Move slowly and be careful not to bend or dent your trim pieces.

14 Once one side is complete, the second side should go faster for you. Use the first side you completed as a reference as you work on the second side.

Roof and Decklid Racks

Stuff a family of four into a Beetle for a road trip and one shortcoming will become painfully obvious within minutes. There's not much room for luggage. That's why roof racks and decklid racks became popular. It's also a popular look with patina rides because you can strap all kinds of accessories to your rack to add personality to your Beetle. Common accessories include vintage suitcases, coolers, surfboards, skateboards, and toys.

There's nothing stopping you from adding both racks to your Beetle, but people usually have just one or the other. The roof rack is more

The over-the-rear-window roof rack was never offered by Volkswagen America. It was a dealer aftermarket add-on available from the late 1960s through the early 1970s. Reproductions are available.

There are many manufacturers of roof racks. Some are more stylish than others. This one is from Vintage Speed in Taiwan. (Photo Courtesy Bryan Bacon)

common than the decklid rack. None of them are standard equipment. That's partially because, as nice as it is to ride without having a suitcase in your lap, racks don't do your car any favors when it comes to efficiency. They reduce your miles per gallon (MPG), often add a lot of wind noise to your ride, and the rack itself can damage your paint surface because the feet and clamp rest right on the paint.

However, if you like the look, they're easy to find nowadays. Many manufacturers make racks now. Most are the old-style metal racks with wood slats. There's even a company making a stainless-steel version that's a bit more streamlined and fits the body lines better than the old style. Most new racks come preassembled. The stainless-steel version typically requires assembly and comes with good instructions from the manufacturer.

Roof Rack Installation

To install your roof rack, start by loosening the two hold-down clamps. Set the rack on the drip rails of your Beetle so that all four feet make contact with the roof. Make sure the rack sits straight on your roof. Open your doors. Then, take the rack's hold-down clamps and slide them underneath the drip rail. Finally, tighten the clamps and you're good to go.

Be sure to check your roof rack on a regular basis to make sure it's still held on tightly and that it's not vibrating loose. Every couple of years, you'll need to sand and refinish the wood if you park your Beetle outside. Also, check the little protective rubber bumpers on the feet periodically. The rubber will break down over time. When you need to replace them, check with the manufacturer or just use bits of 1/4-inch or 5/16-inch fuel line.

Bumpers

Theoretically, your Beetle's bumpers are there for impact protection. Why just theoretically? Well, there are a lot of particulars that come into play that'll determine the extent of damage your Bug would suffer in a collision. It all depends on the impact speed and how hard you hit something.

US-spec bumpers with towel bars were an improvement in safety over the rail-style bumpers coming from Europe at the time. This was a US-only feature.

With the reimagining of how roof racks operate and look, many manufacturers have stepped up to offer more stylish options. They typically fit the body of the car much better. (Photo Courtesy Bryan Bacon)

Early-style bumpers can be added to a late-model Beetle. Some manufacturers make this easy today by providing mounting brackets.

The early bumpers (say, pre-1967) did not offer much crash protection. The later bumpers were stronger, and the Super Beetle bumpers have hydraulic dampeners (like a shock) built in. As federal regulations changed to protect consumers, bumpers got a bit stronger.

Earlier bumpers had a nicer look that was more stylized. That was a designer's work, not an engineer's. As time passed and regulations grew, there was a tradeoff between what looked nice and what was easy, cheap, and compliant.

So, do you really need bumpers? No, especially if you never have a low-speed crash. In a high-speed crash, with or without the bumpers, your crumple zone could mean half of your car gets crunched. Bumpers wouldn't help at all. That means you have some options. However, before you just rip the bumpers off your Beetle and roll, think twice. Some states require vehicles to have bumpers to be deemed roadworthy, even though they offer little protection in a collision.

Some local jurisdictions do not require full bumpers. Bumper guards are permitted in those places. There, these T-bars are perfectly acceptable. (Photo Courtesy Bryan Bacon)

There are many styles of T-bars. Some included a bit of ground-scraping protection just in case you drive over a tall obstruction. (Photo Courtesy Bryan Bacon)

Our experience with fiberglass bumpers is that they are not worth the space they occupy. They offer no protection and only a certain cosmetic appeal if you like them. One reason we don't like fiberglass bumpers despite adding some style is that they tend to delaminate. Since they also add no more protection, they are not an element we like to include.

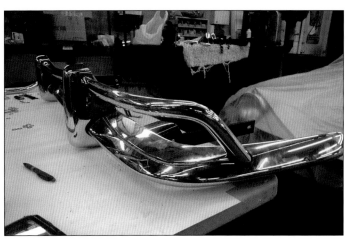

Aftermarket stainless-steel bumpers look nice and wear well. They will require a bit of adjustment to get them to fit correctly.

Stock Volkswagen bumpers were made from heavy-gauge steel and then chromed. They offered 5-mph crash protection, though they sometimes tested better.

If your chrome is in good shape, consider rechroming for cosmetic purposes. You will never find a better fit than you get with the original.

Stock Bumpers

For earlier Beetles, you have two primary options. One is the blade, which is more of a European style. It's just a plain bumper that follows the curve of the front of the car. Beetles sold in Europe came with just the blade.

In the United States, there was a different bumper that came standard, called the towel bar and overriders. There's a style called the T-bar and an even rarer one called the J-bar. There are also fiberglass bumpers available, which is fine if you like the look.

They will do absolutely nothing for you protection-wise; they are only for looks.

Usually, people have matching front and back bumpers. Another popular option is a Euroblade with overriders and no towel bars.

If you spend some time preassembling the bumpers on the bench, installation will be easier. Do not tighten all the fasteners until you have them on the car and adjusted correctly.

Factory Bumpers

The highest-quality bumpers came right from the VW factory. They're made of heavier metal than any you could find in the aftermarket. However, with decades of wear and tear, they're likely to be pitted, rusted, and worn out. As expensive as rechroming is, it still may be the best choice because you will never find bumpers that fit better than those that came from the factory.

The originals had six pieces plus the fasteners for the front. You might get lucky and find some in a junkyard, on an online marketplace, or at a swap meet. Flip the bumper over to look for the VW stamp on the rear side. There's a sort of heft to the originals, as they're made from heavier gauge steel than the aftermarket reproductions.

Bumper Installation

1 Yes, this is a Karmann Ghia with an eight-piece bumper assembly. However, all early Beetles had the same type of assembly. It's best to do a loose fit before tightening everything up.

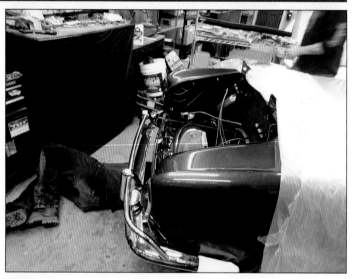

2 After you're happy with the fit, placement, and how it sits on the body, tighten everything up from the inside. Be careful not to scratch your paint in the process.

3 Each individual fastener needs to have Loctite applied and be reset once you have its final location. You don't want anything to work itself loose.

4 When looking at your anodized aluminum car parts, consider whether you should rechrome. This chrome now looks better than it did straight from the factory.

Aftermarket Bumpers

It's easy to find chrome reproductions, but they don't match the quality of the originals. The chrome isn't typically the same high quality, so it won't last as long.

You might also look into stainless-steel reproductions. Mostly produced overseas, the overall quality is good. You'll probably have to wrestle with these bumpers a bit to get them to fit properly without having one side higher than the other.

How to Install Bumpers

It's best to start with a bench assembly rather than wrestling on the floor with your bumpers. Start on the bench to make sure everything fits up loosely. Lay all the parts out on a towel on a table so as not to scratch the finish.

Take the blade and attach one bolt from the blade to the bumper bracket. Do the same to both brackets. Set the first overrider up and attach it loosely to the bumper bracket. Hand tighten the bracket. Slide the center towel bar in at this point. Install the other overrider and hand tighten. Then, slide the outside overriders into the uprights. Bolt it all down through the side of the bumper as well as the upper bolt in the overrider.

Now that you have everything loosely assembled, test fit the bumper on your car. Be very careful not to scratch the paint. A little bit of tape around the body line will be helpful in protecting your finish. Check the profile and height and then the space between the car and bumper edges on both sides. Make sure everything is square, plumb, and true.

If you're happy with how it fits, tighten your bumper brackets to the body. We suggest removing all the fasteners one at a time. Put some Loc-

In customization for your interior, the chrome trim along your dashboard can be color-matched to the car. It's a good way to add a subtle accent.

Dechroming is not for the faint of heart. It involves removing trim, badging, and anything that's shiny. Done right, it looks good.

tite on the threads before reinstalling. Then, tighten all the hardware you previously hand tightened. Tightening properly will prevent road vibration from rattling the nuts loose.

Two More Shiny Bits

Early Beetles (depending on the market, between 1964 and 1968) have a chrome strip that bisects the dash. You can paint, restore, or remove this little bit of bling. You may also have a speedometer bezel, which is a small piece of trim that goes around the gauge.

Low Chrome or No Chrome

Don't like the look of chrome? Want a stealthy, sinister look? Take it off! It's up to you how far you take your chrome disrobing. And yes, it's completely legal.

Debadge That Beetle

What is debadging? Simply put, it's the first stage of dechroming. You remove all the manufacturer's identifying marks from the car, including the hood crest, front emblem, and script on the rear decklid. If it's a convertible, you'll also want to lose the

With the availability of 3D printing and custom manufacturing, anything is possible. Here, we did our logo on the script to make it match the style of what came from the factory (with a twist).

This trim, tires, and wheels had a black undercoat. The car had a white undercoat. But the colors shifted a bit in the sunlight. Don't be afraid to play with different colored primers. (Photo Courtesy Bryan Bacon)

One dechroming option is to paint your headlight rings the same color as the trim or the car body. You can do it as an accent or go with a monochromatic look.

Karmann Ghia badge on the front quarter panel.

Once debadged, you have some choices. Rocking a patina look? Just leave it as is. You could also take it all off, do a little welding and grinding to fill the holes, paint and polish, and continue on your merry way. You could even make a custom badge, emblem, and script to give your Beetle even more personality. Some Volkswagen clubs get badges made for members to purchase. Some owners get custom badges made to suit their tastes.

Dechrome Your Beetle

The next level of Beetle nakedness is dechroming. This means removing all the chrome bits and pieces to get a more subtle or hot-roddy look. A lot of the California-style Bugs and the Gruman look are dechromed.

There are trim-removing tools, plastic spatula-shaped tools that slide under the trim clips and pop them loose. You'll just go around your Bug and remove the trim clips. If the trim clips are plastic, they'll probably break, and you'll need to remove them manually by cutting the heads

off to pop them out. You might need to stick something into the holes to pop the heads out through the back side of the panel.

Side Trim

First, remove the side trim. Deal with the remaining holes for the clips. Some owners get creative with the holes by inserting metal spikes in them to achieve a sinister look. If you want the body smooth, just weld the holes closed and grind them down, then use a hammer and dolly to make the area smooth. Paint and polish.

Rear Script

This bit of chrome is held in with pins and a rubber or metal grommet to attach to the body. Pop the clips off, and you'll be able to lift the script up and out.

Window Seals

Stock Volkswagens in the US market came with chrome trim inserted into the front and rear rubber window seals. You can change the seals out and replace them with Cal-look

With any parts that were chromed at the factory, you'll need to remove the chrome before painting or powder coating. This is a must for good adhesion.

seals, available online or through your VW parts house.

Door Handles

The next piece of chrome to remove is the door handles. Remove them and scuff them up a little before painting or powder coating black or in a color that matches your car. To remove the handles, just unscrew the Phillips-head screw (there may be more than one, depending on your model) in the doorjamb. Then, paint or powder coat and reinstall with the hooked end going in first. Tighten the screw and tuck the door seal back into place.

Front and Rear Latches

Just open the hood or rear decklid. There is either one or two Phillips-head screws to unscrew from the underside of the latch. The latch has an attachment screw and a hook on the top side. Once you remove the screw and unhook the latch from the top, it will slide out.

Pop-Outs

Rear pop-outs were an option when your Beetle was new. If you're installing pop-outs, you can disassemble and then send to powder coat or scuff and paint.

Running Boards

Stock Beetles came with chrome trim on the side of the running board. You can remove this trim. It's attached very much like the body trim, with 10-mm bolts underneath that you'll need to remove. Re-cover your running board with a new rubber cover, available online or at a VW parts store. Just don't install the chrome trim piece when you put it back together. You might also consider swapping your original stock running boards for an aluminum version. They're customizable for color and shine level.

Window Scrapers

The last two chrome bits you might want to change are the outside window scrapers on the front doors and wing window. A good time to change them out is when you'd replace them. The rubber only has a 20- to 30-year life span, so now's a good time to do it. Simply remove, disassemble, scuff and paint or powder coat.

Fix the Holes

If you've removed your Beetle's chrome bits, there are several little holes left behind. Make sure to take care of them so that you don't give corrosion a foothold. You have a little bit of bodywork to erase the evidence of the chrome that used to live on your car. First, weld the holes back up, then grind the welds smooth before priming and painting.

You can include a third brake light for additional customization. You'll need to weld and do some bodywork to make it look right.

WEIRD BUG BODIES

To anyone else, your Beetle might look like a car. The four wheels, two doors, seats, and a steering wheel are to blame for that misconception. Sure, it's transportation, but to the most adventurous Bug owners, the Type 1 is so much more. A veritable blank canvas begging for customization, it would take more than a lifetime to build all the versions of the Beetle that our imaginations can conjure.

We've discussed several systems and components that Beetle owners can't stop tinkering with in the quest to give their ride extra personality. However, those modifications pale in comparison with what we're going to discuss now.

What follows is an imagination-stretching array of radical modifications that you could make to your Beetle, from least to most extreme. The novice in the air-cooled Volkswagen world might stare, point, and wonder what exactly they're seeing.

Subtle modifications, including lowering and narrowing the front suspension and putting on a nice set of aftermarket rims, can definitely improve the look of your ride. Plus, these modifications are easy to make.

Whether in the desert or running on the sand dunes, Bajas provide great grip and ground clearance as you drive in the wild. You're ready for an adventure if you have one. (Photo Courtesy Eric Arnold)

Just because you can think it doesn't mean you should do it. Think about the modifications you're making for your Bug. If you're doing it because you like it, great. It may not be what anyone else likes, and that's fine.

The Beetle chassis lends itself to some radical modifications. Suicide doors and aftermarket rims can either make or break your ride's look. Do what you like.

But whether you run with any of these ideas or not, you'll know what they are and how they were done.

Suicide Doors

For such a friendly looking little car, it might seem nearly obscene to make a modification with such a sinister name. The gruesome moniker belies the glamorous origins of this door setup in which the door hinges at the rear rather than from the front.

Once called "French doors," this door style evoked the image of fancy people wearing fancy clothes, gracefully exiting a carriage with the help of a footman. Off for an evening at the opera, these fine folks found it easier to get out of a carriage by stepping frontward rather than having to plant one foot on the ground, scoot to the edge of the seat, and then turn around to get out of the path of the door. Ladies of old had double the trouble of getting in and out of their transportation because of their long gowns and impractical footwear.

For any parent who's wrestled to install an infant car seat in the rear of the typical four-door car, the idea of a rear-hinged door might sound like the best invention since the baby monitor. Perhaps today's minivans with their automatic sliding doors answered that cry for help.

As ideal as these doors may sound, given their original design intention, there is a reason that they received their nickname: suicide doors. Some four-door cars of old that sported this door configuration had no B-pillar. Open the front and rear doors and recline your front seats, and you could practically pass a Ping-Pong table through the opening. They are pretty, spacious, and elegant, but this engineering design left something to be desired when it came to safety.

Then, there was the possibility of aerodynamics wrenching such a door open while traveling at full speed. Plus, if you've ever watched an old gangster movie, you can imagine how the prospect of discharging pas-

sengers without even slowing down might go.

Given the fact that few passengers back in the day had much use for seat belts, this unfortunate physics experiment was likely to leave an unwitting passenger suddenly having a personal introduction to the asphalt. Add in the increased probability of a passenger opening their suicide door into oncoming traffic and getting killed, and it's no wonder why very few new vehicles have rear-hinged doors. However, several Rolls-Royce models and a few other outliers still feature their euphemistically named "coach" doors.

Gruesome history aside, this is a pretty cool modification that you could make to your Beetle relatively inexpensively and easily. If you're not already drawing enough stares from passersby as you tool around in your Bug, their jaws will undoubtedly drop when they watch you exit the vehicle in such a civilized manner.

Reversing the Doors

While you certainly could entrust your Bug to a shop that specializes in air-cooled Volkswagen body modifications and restorations, this is a customization you can do on your own if you can weld, use a cutting wheel, and follow instructions. Several aftermarket parts manufacturers sell complete suicide door conversion kits, which will help eliminate some of the guesswork you'd face if you just did this entirely on your own.

The process of relocating hinges and the hinge pockets is relatively straightforward. Remove the factory latching mechanisms and hinge pins in your doorjamb. Then, determine where the new hinge pockets will go. This is most definitely a case for "measure twice, cut once," so think this through. The hinge pocket location will determine where the hinges attach to the door, so be sure your placement takes the window channel and door design into account.

The farther apart you can place the hinges, the sturdier your door will be because you'll decrease the amount of flex in the structure. It's also best to put your hinge placement as close to the outside of the Beetle as possible so that you don't fling your door open and dent your car's body.

It's also important to make sure that your hinge assembly is perpendicular to the ground. You'll also want to be aware of your doors' innards before cutting anything. Just remove your door panel so you can see what you're doing.

Tack weld the door end of the hinge into the door itself. A dozen tack welds will do the trick. Then, you can test the door. If you like the result, keep going. If not, correct your placement before going any further. Once the door fits right, remove the factory pins and hinges and bolt the new hinges into the door pockets.

Mount your new door hinge pockets in the doorjamb, being sure to cut the opening to match the pocket as perfectly as you can. You don't want your door hinge security relying on a sloppy cut that's "corrected" with a weld. It's better to cut a small hole and file it larger to fit perfectly than to cut a hole that's too large and end up trying to correct it.

Door Latch Installation

The perfect placement for the new latch is where it will connect with the striker and the striker plate on the doorjamb. Your kit may have a template to make this easy. If not, make a template yourself by placing the latch where you want it and tracing around the install plate.

Check your work, and if everything lines up, check it once more for good measure. Then, bolt your new latch (often called a bear claw latch) to the install plate, then weld it into place.

Striker Plate and Strike Pin Installation

Now, you'll align the strike pin. Latch it, then climb into your Beetle and close the door. Note the location on the doorjamb where the strike plate should go. Spot weld the striker plate onto the jamb. Attach the striker pin to the plate and close the door to test its placement again.

If the door operates smoothly, weld the striker plate into position.

Depending on your welding skills, you may have more or less cleanup work to do to prepare the door for paint.

Once you finish the suicide door modification, enjoy the look of awe as you enter and exit your Beetle. Also, wear your seat belt and be sure to check your surroundings carefully before opening your door.

Shaved Door Handles

For the ultimate in sleek and clean body lines, you could shave your door handles off. This process involves removing the exterior door handles, then welding the holes and all the bodywork that comes from removing parts. You'll need to apply primer, surfacer, paint, and clear.

You can buy a door popper kit with a latch release pull. After all, you still need to get in and out of the car. You'll also need some additional wiring to power it all. Your friendly local auto parts store can order a kit for you, or you can order one online for yourself.

The instructions for installation vary by manufacturer, so be sure to follow them closely. You may also need to do a bit more or less fabrication, depending on the style of poppers and pullers.

Note, this is a rather advanced modification. You'll need to be comfortable doing bodywork and have a solid understanding of 12-volt electrical systems, including microswitches, relays, and wiring. There is some fabrication involved.

If you worry about being locked out of your car if you lose power or your battery is drained, don't fret. You'll install a manual cable pull running through the rear of the front fender well. To activate it, just pull the cable and open your door.

Shaving the Door Handles

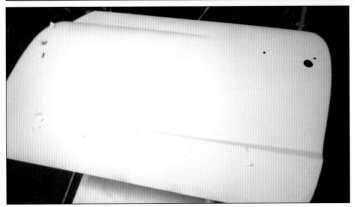

1 Start with a stock door. After blasting the paint off, seal the fresh door panel with an epoxy sealer to prevent corrosion while you're working on the doors.

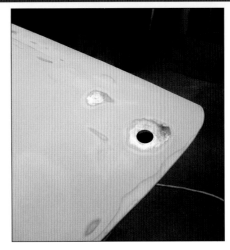

2 Weld smaller holes up and grind them back to flush and smooth. This is straight enough for doing the bodywork.

3 For larger holes, cut plugs from old pieces of sheet metal. Fit them to size. The closer you can get it to be just under the size of the hole, the easier it will be to finish.

4 After getting it to the rough size, using the hole as a gauge, do a bit of grinding on the edges to make it fit perfectly. The plug should be 1/32 inch smaller than the diameter of the hole.

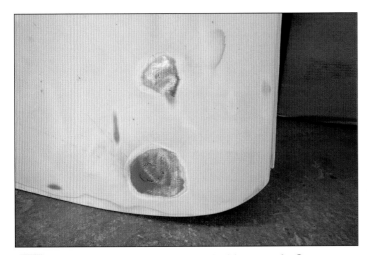

5 Weld the surface up and grind it smooth. Once you do that, it's time for a bit of minor filler work to the areas you just welded.

6 Apply a heavy coat of epoxy primer. That will seal the filler work, bare steel, and primer. You want a stable surface for paint to adhere to.

Shaving the Door Handles *continued*

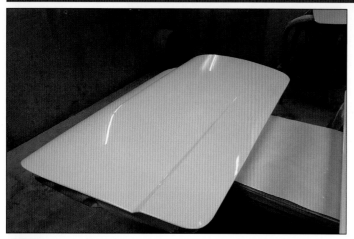

7 *Shoot the color and clear. Buff it to shine. Now, the door is ready to install back onto your car.*

8 *You can see on this door we installed that the appearance is smooth, sleek, and sexy. With no interruption of chrome, the look is eye-catching.*

Baja Beetles

Far less grim sounding than the suicide doors, the Baja modification sounds like you're in for a wild, grin-inducing, probably bouncy ride. The same goes for actually driving one.

Baja Bugs are perfect for driving on off-road adventures, whether it's on the beach, in the desert, or racing up and down sand dunes. The first

Baja burst onto the Beetle scene in 1968, when Gary Emory ripped half the body off his Bug, raised it, and exposed its engine in response to the dune buggy craze.

They're loud because they have no muffler. They're half-naked because they have no aprons or fenders. They're raised to allow for better ground clearance. And for Bajas that race, they're lighter than regular Beetles because they're stripped down.

There's nothing extra on board: no back seats, no floor mats, no heater, and no rear decklid.

Of course, you can find Bajas to buy, but if you have a daily driver you'd like to convert, it's a pretty good project for a novice to complete. You could probably do it in a weekend or two. To build a Baja Beetle, you'll need a Beetle, of course. But otherwise, all you really need are:

Originally designed for the Baja 500 and for the beach, these rides are stylistically coming into their own. They're able to roll over rough terrain at 60 mph without a problem. (Photo Courtesy Eric Arnold)

Bajas might look different from most VW Beetles, but the extra cooling coming from the upper shrouds and the exhaust gases being piped away from the engine make sure that your Bug runs nice and cool. (Photo Courtesy Eric Arnold)

Tools Required

Gather the following tools and equipment:
- Floor jack
- Jack stands (4)
- Socket set
- Ratchet
- Sawzall
- Sprint bars
- Jigsaw
- Big hammer
- Chisel
- Grinder
- Painter's tape
- Safety glasses

Disassembly

Frankly, building a Baja is much more a matter of un-building a Beetle. Jack it up and rest your Bug on jack stands. Take the wheels off. Then, take the decklid off by removing the bolts that connect the hinges to the body. Remove the rear bumper, rear fenders, and running boards next by removing the bolts that hold them all on.

Behold the lifted stance of the Baja Beetle. They're intended to go off-road, so they need greater ground clearance.

Bajas have larger rims and tires plus fiberglass fenders that are shorter than stock. It's all to give better off-road performance.

Baja engines are usually exposed. Typically, the exhaust comes up out of the top of the engine so it doesn't drag on the ground.

Some Baja owners add LED lights for off-roading as well as custom-made tubular bumpers. Notice that the headlights have been relocated to inside the fenders, also made of fiberglass.

With bigger rims and tires, you will have a reduction in gearing. The bigger the tire, the slower it rotates, which is great for off-road driving.

Typically, Bajas feature roll bars as a safety measure. They also usually have three- to five-point harnesses to keep you in the seat on bumpy rides.

Some Baja owners want to ride even higher. We have installed a 3-inch lift kit on this one to give more ground clearance, per the owner's request.

Rip out the wiring to the tail-lights. Pull out the throttle cable that goes to the carburetor. Unbolt the engine tin while you're at it. The rear apron comes off too, thanks to your Sawzall. If you feel like Godzilla ripping your Beetle to pieces, perhaps you're being a bit overzealous, but you're on the right track.

Be careful with the next step, no matter how hyped up you are from all that deconstruction. The engine needs to come out. It's bolted to the gearbox. There's also a crossmember at the rear of the engine bay that's holding it in. Engines are heavier than they look, even if you're amped up on adrenaline. It's best to ask a friend to help with that step.

Rebuilding Phase

Now, reshape your fenders. Mark the shape you want with painter's tape. Remember that you need to leave sufficient bolt holes intact so that you can bolt the fender back onto the body. Use a jigsaw to cut away any bits of the fender that are not wanted.

Inside the engine bay, there are welds in the channel that hold the engine to the body gasket. Use a chisel, hammer, and Sawzall to remove that material. Your grinder will work wonders for cleaning up the cuts you just made. With a Baja, using rattle-can paint is perfectly acceptable. These are workhorses, not trailer queens.

Paint the inside of the engine bay so that any exposed metal is now protected. Reinstall the engine, rewire the taillights, and reconnect the throttle cable to the carburetor. Put the wheels back on, and carefully lower your new Baja to the ground. You're in for an adventure now!

Rat Rods

Here's another fairly quick and dirty modification you can make to your Beetle. Of course, you wouldn't want to do this to a beautifully restored Bug, but it makes a great project for a beater or two if you want to get creative.

Rat rods are in the lineage of hot rods with one characteristic feature. They look like they should not possibly be able to hold themselves together. They're old and beat-up

Rat rods come in all shapes and forms, whether they are patina rides or hot rods. Only your imagination is stopping you from creating something truly unique to drive.

looking. They're usually fast. They also make the perfect weekend project. Oh, and if a part falls off or wears out, all that is required is to go to your favorite junkyard to find a replacement that you can make work.

"Build" is too strong of a word for this project. It's more a matter of deconstructing, reconfiguring, and getting creative with the parts. Start by stripping your Beetle's interior and draining the gas tank for safety. It may be easier to remove the engine than to try to work around it.

You can modify your frame, adjusting where the axles and wheels go. Just use a reciprocating saw and a welder to make any modification from your imagination. When you're finished customizing your rat's body, weld it to the frame.

Once the body is as you wish, start rebuilding. Reinstall the engine. Install the brakes. Add seats for yourself and a passenger. Maybe spring for some new tires while you're at it, just for safety's sake.

All that's left now is to prepare yourself for stares and comments every single time you take your rat rod out in public. People won't believe their eyes, and you'll hear the same questions over and over. Maybe your ride will inspire them to build their own.

VW Rails

We're going off-road again with a popular modification that is hard for non-VW people to believe is based on the Beetle. Built specifically for rough and sandy terrain, this custom vehicle has very little body. Instead, it's essentially a seat or two welded to a bare-bones frame, strapped to a speedy drivetrain. The rear placement of the engine makes for excellent

Sometimes the best views in life come through a plexiglass windshield with nothing ahead but sand or mud. It's time to go out in nature to have some fun.

The heaviest parts of your rail are your engine and transmission, which make for great traction. These beasts will get up and go when more civilized rides are stuck in the garage.

Off-road rails can be made street legal with a few modifications to comply with state regulations. The main reason for rails is to go out and have some fun leaving the roads behind.

traction. Throw in a strong suspension, wheels, tires, a steering wheel, and brakes, and you're good to go. Again, this would make a good weekend (or two) project.

If you're a skilled welder, you may enjoy building your rail frame. If not, they are available from many online sources. Essentially, you'll be driving around in a roll cage, so rails are not necessarily as dangerous as they appear.

Depending on your state law, yours may or may not be street legal. The laws may be a bit perplexing, though. For example, in Alabama, your vehicle does not have to have a windshield to be street legal. But it must have windshield wipers. Think about that for a moment.

Beetle Dune Buggies

Not to be confused with rails, the dune buggy is their family friendly cousin. Two-seaters are built on a shortened Beetle chassis and topped with a fiberglass body of sorts. Four-seaters are even simpler, as they use an unmodified chassis. Either way, buggies are the ultimate kit car. Bruce Meyers, of Meyers Manx fame, started designing his buggy bodies in 1964.

Originally intended for driving at the beach or in other sandy locations, this open-air vehicle is actually street legal in many states. Again, check your local laws to avoid unwanted encounters with law enforcement.

The easiest way to Buggy your Beetle is to buy a ready-made fiberglass kit. You'll need a buggy buddy to do this project safely, at least for some parts of the process.

If you're building a two-seater and need to shorten your chassis, you'll find it easier to work on if you remove the engine first. If you're building a four-seater, that's not as important. Either way, detach and remove the battery for safety.

Disconnect all the wiring you can get to now and consider upgrading to a new wiring harness while you have the vehicle taken apart. Wires don't last forever, after all.

To start, you'll remove your Beetle's body from the chassis. Jack it up and place it securely on jack stands so you can get underneath safely. Un-mating the body and the pan is as easy as unbolting the series of 22 17-mm bolts holding it together. They run along the sides and then along the crossbeam under the back seat area.

Remove the fuel tank, fuel line, and brake fluid lines. Then, remove every component possible from your Beetle. Be careful to check for wiring as you remove each component. Bag, tag, label, and take photos of your progress so you can find all the little bits you plan to reuse later.

There are many manufacturers of dune buggy bodies. But there are a few out there that stand out from the crowd. This is a Meyers Manx body.

Two-seater bodies are another fun way to enjoy the Volkswagen hobby. They were originally designed to go on the beach and in the surf, but now you can see them on trails everywhere.

Buggy Building

1 Here's a prime example of a VW chassis waiting to be recycled into its new life as a dune buggy. Lots of fun awaits the owner of any vehicle that can go off-road.

2 With the body removed, start stripping the pan to get it ready for a dune buggy body. To save money, reuse your suspension and brakes.

3 With a group of four or five buddies, pulling the body off is fairly easy. After everything is unbolted, the body comes off the pan.

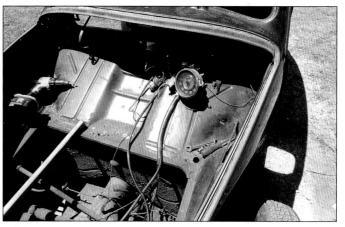

4 If you are recycling your electrical system, tag, bag, and mark every connection as you disassemble the wiring harness. We suggest upgrading to a new harness while you're in there.

5 Continue disassembling the chassis. The motor, transmission, and brake lines come out. Remove everything from your pan before sending it through blasting.

6 What to do with the yard art? Our suggestion would be to put the body up for sale online. Someone out there is restoring a true classic and is looking for that body right now.

Buggy Building *continued*

7 With the pan disassembled, you can now do a thorough inspection for rust. All the corrosion you see needs to be fixed, and now is the time to do it.

8 At this point, it's a good time to clean up all the inserts and capture nuts. By taking care of them now, reassembly will be a lot easier when the time comes.

9 While your chassis is off, this is a good time to repair any broken parts inside the tunnels. It sure beats losing a clutch cable tube while you're driving.

10 Always inspect for rust. Replace metal as necessary. You want a nice, strong foundation for your buggy.

11 With a shortened pan, you have to shorten the floor pan as well as the tunnel for the two-seater buggy. While you can make it look like it came from the factory that way, that's not necessary. Just make sure everything fits.

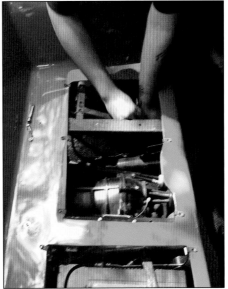

12 In dune buggies, battery access can be limited. Some have the battery under the back seat to make it easier to get to when needed.

While you have a friend handy, remove your Beetle's frame from the chassis. It's heavy, so you might actually want to enlist the help of multiple friends. Four should do the trick. Once you have the body off, you could part it out or turn it into some kitschy automotive art that'll make you the envy of the neighborhood.

With the body off the chassis, inspect for rust. If your chassis is in pristine condition, great. But that's not likely. If there is rust, you'll need to address it. The best practice is to get the pan sandblasted so you can really see its condition. The less expensive but more labor-intensive option would be to hand-sand or chemically strip it.

If you have rust, it must be cut out and replaced. That will involve welding. You can either take this as an opportunity to practice and improve your welding skills or you can take the chassis to a shop that can fix it for you.

If you're building a two-seater, you'll need to shorten your chassis. Simply follow the specifications that come with your kit. If you're building

There are many ways to do a Bug old school versus this updated and fresh look. (Photo Courtesy Pete Skiba)

Chopped, wearing suicide doors, and no fender, this Bug makes a nice hot rod and draws admiring stares wherever it goes. (Photo Courtesy Eric Fernon)

a four-seater, you are ready to start rebuilding now.

Install your Beetle engine on the back of the dune buggy, behind the seats, according to the kit's instructions. Then, install the battery. Now is a good time to upgrade it. If you prefer a smoother ride over a teeth-jarring one, install shocks. Now is a good time to invest in new tires, too. Then, it's time to fit your fiberglass buggy body over the chassis. The kits include everything you need, including manufacturer-specific instructions. Get it all bolted up and head to the beach for the time of your life.

Chopped Bugs

We've finally arrived at the most radical of Bug body modifications: the chop. At first glance, if you're going fast enough, passersby may not even notice that something's different about your Beetle. But once they have the chance to study the lines, or if they see your Bug next to one that hasn't been modified like this, there

will be no doubt in their minds. Your Beetle's dimensions will be utterly customized. In general, chopped Bugs are shorter in stature, and while they may appear shorter front to back, it's often an optical illusion.

This is not a project for the faint of heart. You will need excellent measuring, math, welding, and grinding skills to pull off the perfect chop. Essentially, you'll chop the roof right off your Beetle to shorten your pillars. Then, you'll need to reshape your roof to make it fit. Many chopped rides actually use multiple roofs to create the new one.

We spoke with Eric Fernon, who built a chopped Beetle with his brother-in-law, Steven Hawkins. Eric is a designer and a professional automotive photographer. Steven is an engineer. Together, they made the perfect team for building this project. It took them one Bug they bought for $140, seven long years of working on it one weekend day per week, and a whole lot of trial and error as they made this radical body look as if it

came from the factory that way.

As Eric puts it, "It's just metal. If you screw up, you can cut it apart and do it again." This project will take epic levels of patience. The duo made four attempts to get the driver-side door right. Its suicide doors required tight tolerances.

This is the type of build where the more you look at it, the more modifications you'll notice. They stretched their Beetle by 10.5 inches and shortened its height by 4 inches and used a single roof to do it. The windshield is a custom-built safari window. The dashboard is from a 1959 Volkswagen bus.

If you go looking for the fuse panel in its usual spot, you won't find it. It's been relocated to a spot underneath the back seat with all its wires hidden. They were aiming for an old dragster look, and they did it.

Far from being a trailer queen, this chopped Beetle gets serious road use. In fact, Eric drives it more often than his other car. Whenever he's on the road, onlookers lose their minds. He says little kids think it's a Hot Wheels car. For older folks, Eric's car brings back memories of hot rods from generations past.

No matter where he goes, people tell him their Volkswagen stories. To Eric, that's the whole point—it's a great conversation starter. Would he ever do it again? Well, let's just say it was a labor of love.

In the end, even if you leave your Beetle's body mostly intact rather than making any of these major modifications, you can appreciate the innovation and imagination that go into such a project. The fact that there are so many radical customizations that Beetle owners have made over the years just reinforces the idea that these are, indeed, the blank canvas of cars.

ELECTRICAL AND LIGHTING

Do you like being able to go, see, be seen, and know what's going on with your Beetle? Who doesn't? We can thank the electrical system for these safety features. There are important electrical considerations that every classic Beetle owner should consider.

Primarily, be sure that your wiring is in tip-top shape as a matter of regular maintenance. Old wires degrade with time as the rubber coating thins and becomes brittle.

Vintage Bug owners often find that the source of various electrical gremlins is nothing more than some "creative" wiring. Shoddy wiring can cause all kinds of strange results, including headlights that won't stay lit, horns that sound when the wipers are activated, unintentionally heated seats when you put a bag of groceries in just the wrong spot, and more.

If you're planning on a pan-off restoration for your Beetle, that's your golden opportunity to replace your wiring harness. Even if you leave the pan on, a wiring upgrade is worth the automotive yoga session required to ensure that your electrical system is up to snuff. You can learn more in CarTech's *How to Restore Your Volkswagen Beetle*.

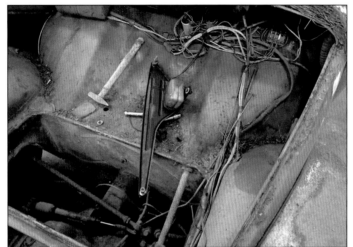

This 1952 VW wiring harness has seen better days. During the thousands of electrical cycles, the insulation has broken down and is starting to cause shorts. This is dangerous.

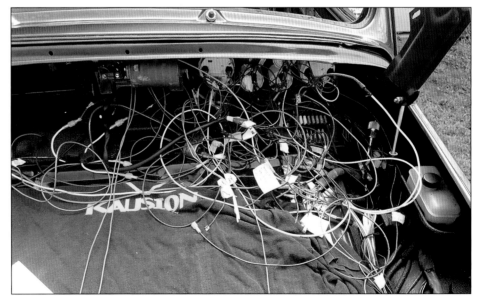

Creative wiring gone bad here. While it might work, there is no sense in trying to troubleshoot this mess. It is better to rip it out and start over.

There are many manufacturers of wiring harnesses that'll work just fine. There are stock kits and custom kits with all the bells and whistles.

Don't be afraid to climb into your work. Automotive yoga is a must for being able to see what you're working on. Make sure you stretch first.

However, even once your wiring is sorted, there is more fun to be had when it comes to electricity. Let's look at some common electrical and lighting modifications that you might want to make on your Beetle.

Batteries

The two main types of car batteries are lead-acid batteries and gel batteries. The gel version is relatively new and designed to require less maintenance. It is filled with a gel electrolyte instead of the traditional battery acid.

Gel batteries are sealed tightly, making a spill nearly impossible. They're also considerably lighter than lead-acid batteries. They hold a charge longer and are less likely to fail in cold weather.

On the downside, gel batteries can be significantly more expensive on the initial purchase. However, as they last longer, their overall cost per year of use is lower. The other drawback to gel batteries is that if you live in a hot climate, they may not fare so well, so you could be looking at a shorter service life.

Lighting

Headlights, taillights, turn signals, parking lights, city lights,

Automotive wiring can take a long time to do. The goal is getting it all to work, but it's just as important to make it look neat as well. A wiring harness can help.

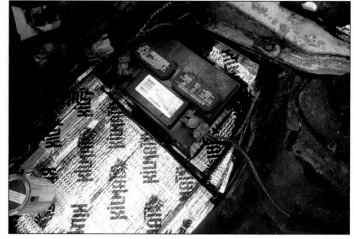

For a lead-acid battery, this is a pretty good value. It will last three to five years. But it is subject to boil over and degrading over time.

You can eliminate your factory courtesy light by not wiring it, then padding over the existing holes. Run your headliner with no cutouts.

LEDs are a drop-in replacement. While the glass curvature isn't quite period correct, the light is far superior to what came from the factory.

Fog lamps come in a variety of sizes and wattages. You can't go wrong by choosing one with 175 watts in an LED.

We installed an LED light. Notice the flat profile of the glass. This light will last about three to five times longer than the bulbs that came from the factory, and it produces cleaner light.

running lights, and interior lights serve important safety purposes: they let you see where you're going and other drivers see you. However, these lights also provide an easy opportunity for customization. The range of lights available now can be overwhelming with different sizes, types, and styles readily available.

You might consider projector headlights with laser-focused beams. There are also DRL bar headlights, which can provide a futuristic look. Then, there are LED lights, which are super-durable, long-lasting, brighter, cool to the touch, energy efficient, and hard to rattle loose.

You could also play around with fog lights, light covers, and various styles. LED lights, in particular, come in a wide range of colors. This opens a whole new world of possibilities, particularly for in-cabin lighting.

Best of all, in most cases, swapping incandescent lights for LEDs is as simple as removing the old and plugging in the new. As LED lights are still relatively expensive to buy compared with incandescents, it's a plus to know you don't have to replace them all at once, making this a budget-friendly upgrade.

Headlights

To start, the headlights are the easiest to modify, and they will also make the biggest impact. Replacing

HID headlights are the next step up from Edison bulbs. They run a bit hotter and draw more amperage than stock, but they give a much cleaner light.

the headlights is a rather straightforward process. The biggest challenge you may face is if your screws have gotten rusty or stripped.

First, identify which light style you like. There are versions with curved glass, flat glass, and those with built-in turn signals too. Halogen bulbs are a nice upgrade. The next level includes LED bulbs, which are an even better upgrade, if pricey. Then, there are high-intensity discharge (HID) bulbs, which come in many colors and are relatively inexpensive, but they take a bit longer to install.

If you've added a high-powered sound system to your Beetle, you may have power considerations to take into account. In that case, LED and HID bulbs are the way to go.

LED Light Installation

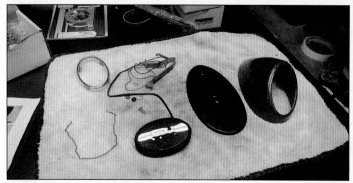

1 *Lay all of the materials out that you will need to install the lights. This way you will know you have all the parts and that they are clean, polished, intact, and/or painted.*

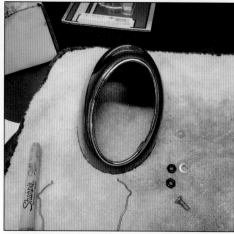

2 *Install the chrome trim ring into the taillight housing. There are four tabs that need to be bent inward before installing, then bent back outward to accept the retaining spring.*

3 *Slide your LED headlight into the trim ring, installing the spring retainer. Do the upper retainer clips before doing the lower retainer clips.*

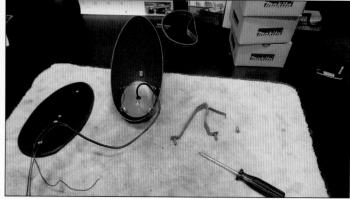

4 *Next, install the mounting bracket into the taillight housing. It's a stainless-steel Phillips screw going into the mounting bracket.*

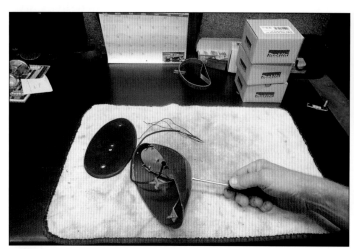

5 *The screw is threaded through the taillight housing into the bracket. At this point, just hand-tighten rather than screwing it tightly.*

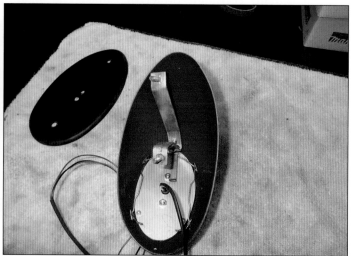

6 *Put the bracket in place with the retailing screw. Don't tighten it yet. Now, it's ready for installing the rubber gasket.*

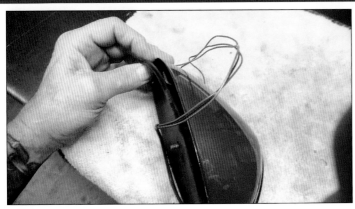

7 *The taillight gasket needs to be stretched over the taillight housing with the two studs protruding to the outside of the gasket. Make sure the gasket goes around the lip of the housing completely.*

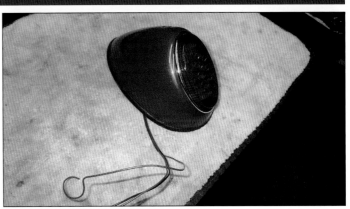

8 *With all the preassembly finished, it's ready to install onto the fender. The gasket is liable to slip off the upper or lower section, so make sure to keep it on the lip.*

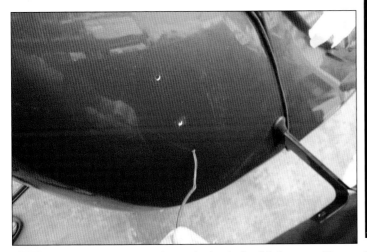

9 *Thread the wiring through the hole. Make sure there is no binding or crimping of the wires, and don't let the wires get scraped on their way in.*

10 *There are two studs coming through. Wavy washers are installed first. Attach the upper nut loosely.*

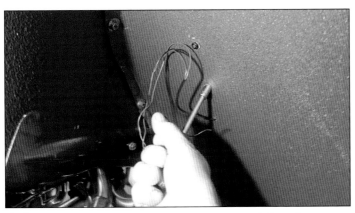

11 *Install the lower nut next. Torque to 6 ft-lbs of torque. Don't snap the studs off by overtightening them.*

12 *Tighten both nuts to 6 ft-lbs. A little bit of Loctite will be helpful. This is a vibration-sensitive panel.*

LED Light Installation

13 *This taillight is installed. As it is tightened, go back and check your seal to make sure it's fitting correctly around the lip of the taillight section.*

14 *After you get one side done, start the other side. Follow the same procedure. Make sure the taillights are plumb to the car.*

Interior Lights

If you want to upgrade your interior lights, the dome light is likely the easiest place to start because it's the easiest to access. You just remove the bulb cover or lens and clean it. Take the bulb with you to your friendly local auto parts store (or shop online), and choose a bulb that's compatible with the original and its connector.

When you install the replacement, note that there's likely a positive and negative side to the bulb. Install accordingly, and put the lens

Courtesy floor lights can be done in LED in multiple colors to fit the theme of your ride. Since this car is red and black, we chose red cabin lighting.

Factory location for the VW Beetle courtesy light. If you're doing an LED conversion, simply pull the plastic cover off, remove the Edison bulb, and install the LED.

This 1968 Euro Beetle has green cabin lighting to match its color theme. Colored cabin lighting can give extra customization to any Beetle.

cover back in place. Another option is to delete your dome light and install LED strip lighting on your cabin floor. There are many colors available to match your ride.

Gauge Lighting

Not all lights are meant for seeing the road or being seen by other drivers. The Volkswagen factory was a bit stingy on gauges. The early models had little more than a speedometer. The fuel gauge came later.

VDO makes period-correct aftermarket gauges to monitor other vital systems never covered by the original manufacturer. This one shows the cylinder head temperature and oil pressure.

If your vehicle did not come with a fuel gauge, VDO makes a customizable version. It comes in electrical and mechanical models, so choose the one that matches your sender.

Modern drivers often want more information than how fast they're going and how soon they'll need to stop for fuel. That's why aftermarket suppliers also sell rev counters, volt meters, oil temperature gauges, and amp meters that can be retrofitted into originally sparsely populated dashboards. Of course, being able to read these gauges in the dark is just as important as being able to see them during the daytime.

You can switch to LED or incandescent options. The Edison-style bulb is what came from the factory. With an LED, you can get different colors, which can make for a nice custom touch.

Disconnect your power first, for safety. In the gauges, there is a recessed hole that the bulb holder slides into. Simply pull that out and change the bulb. Then, slide it back in.

You can send your original speedometer out for a custom rebuild. They can zero the mileage out and make it look brand new, but it will still perform like it did from the factory.

Aftermarket manufacturers are recreating a fully modern LED screen speedometer. It can be calibrated to your ride to give an accurate reading.

Tachometers are a good gauge to add. If you can find one, the 914 gauge is almost a direct fit into the Beetle's dashboard. It's pretty much plug and play.

Beep Beep!

There's nothing quite like the distinctive sound of a Beetle's horn, and yet, some owners want to add a little custom touch by changing it. You will find all kinds of sounds and even musical horns available online.

This is a fairly easy modification to make, as it involves only one bolt and two electrical connections. The horn is typically mounted underneath the front fender in front of the tire. Swap out the horn, then be sure to test it.

Generator to Alternator Upgrade

If you have serious gadget cravings for your Beetle and those frills are too much for your original electrical system's generator to handle, or if you have a hard time keeping your battery juiced and find yourself jumping your Bug more often than you'd like, you can upgrade from a generator to an alternator.

In short, here's the difference between the two. A generator creates direct current. An alternator creates alternating current. They both generate electricity; they just operate differently.

An alternator works as a charging system that produces electricity by converting mechanical energy into electrical energy that charges the car battery. The mechanical energy rotates a magnet, producing magnetic flux to produce electrical current.

Alternators are efficient energy producers, generating electricity only when needed. The primary drawback with an alternator is that it can't charge a battery that's completely dead. Also, if your alternator produces too much or too little voltage, you can damage your battery and other electrical stuff in your Beetle. (Alternators are fitted with voltage regulators, so that's usually not a problem.)

A generator converts mechanical energy into electrical energy too. But it does so with coiled wires inside a magnetic field. The coiled wires rotate, generating power. The magnet stays still; it's the rotating wires that generate electricity. Generators can charge a dead battery, and they produce direct current.

If you want to make the move from generator to alternator, the first question to answer is whether you have a 6-volt or 12-volt electrical system. That's going to determine where your regulator is. For a 6-volt system, the regulator is located on top of the generator. With a 12-volt, it's under the rear passenger seat. In this case, you'll connect your Beetle's main power wires together (they're thick) and then your gauge signal wires (they're thin).

You'll need to get an alternator conversion kit, which includes an alternator, alternator stand, a 12-volt alternator belt, backing plates, and a 12-volt pulley. You can choose between a 55-amp and 70-amp alternator. If you have an air-ride system or a major sound system, go with 70 amps.

Determine which wire leads to the speedometer's alternator charging bulb. It should connect to the 10-mm threaded nut on top of the alternator. The other wire just connects to the positive node on your battery.

Pictured is a 6-volt generator dynamo. If your generator is working well, keep it until it fails. Then, it's easy to change out the voltage regulator, which is the part likely to fail.

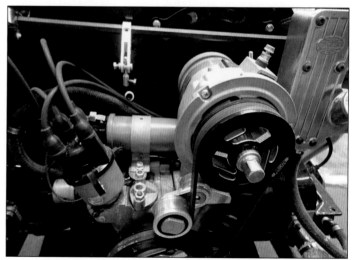

By upgrading to an alternator, you have the option to go from 65 watts to 110 watts with an upgrade. This will help keep your battery topped off and ready to go.

Currently, the best battery pack on the market for electric conversions is the Tesla battery system. You may or may not need to add a cooling system.

The rear battery bank is a good place to mount your controller and interface panels. You will have to upholster and cover this area later if you want to hide it.

Electric Conversions

This is a big project, and it won't be cheap. Plus, obviously, you will lose the trademark "can full of pebbles" sound that is typical of classic Volkswagens. However, some Beetle owners want to convert their rides into EV versions.

The Beetle is a good candidate in some ways. It's a lightweight vehicle, which will help extend its travel range on a charge and increase its energy efficiency. It also has a lot of room for the bank of multiple batteries needed to run the engine.

Typically, with an EV Beetle conversion, the battery banks go under the seats and in the cargo compartment. The Beetle's chassis is also comparatively strong, which is important because those batteries add a few hundred extra pounds to the car's weight, even minus the transmission, full fuel tank, and gasoline engine. Of course, be sure your Beetle is structurally sound and not riddled with rust.

Components involved in the conversion include the motor, the converter or controller, and the batteries. The batteries drive the bulk of the cost of your conversion, as you want the very best you can afford to buy. They'll determine how long it takes to charge your Bug and how far you can go. But remember, you will

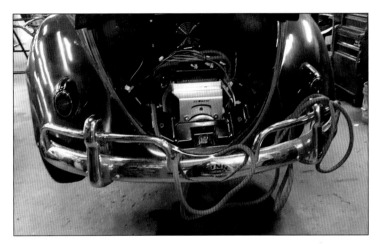

There are a whole lot of high-voltage cables required with an electric conversion. In fact, it requires nearly 26 feet of cable.

likely need to replace them within two to five years, depending on how often you drive and how much demand you put on them. While it's fun to put pedal to metal, that instant torque will take a toll.

While this technology is still evolving, each iteration of the components seems to be better than the last. Currently, there are no kits we can recommend. It's not a project well-suited for a hobbyist because you'll need to be proficient in electrical engineering and mechanically inclined. However, there are shops that specialize in electrical conversions. You'll pay a pretty penny for their expertise. However, if you are determined to make this modification, it's definitely possible.

There will be some electrical connections under the battery tray to connect the motor to the regulators to the controllers to the charging system and finally to the battery pack.

RAGTOP CONVERSIONS

The only delight in life that tops the feeling of cruising a tree-lined, curvy road in your Volkswagen Beetle is to do so in a ragtop conversion. Not as windy as a top-down convertible but still with a gentle stream of fresh air and sunshine landing on you as you drive, the ragtop evolution was destined to happen.

This modification began gaining traction in the 1950s and 1960s when someone, somewhere replaced their original roof with a sunroof. Maybe it was rigged together; maybe aftermarket parts were cobbled together to make it work.

Even with the company's stern dedication to efficiency and simplicity, the engineers at Volkswagen must have had a soft spot for feeling the wind in their hair. In 1950, the carmaker began offering full-roof fabric tops. Some say they mimicked the 1937 Nash sedan's top.

Whether tilting, sliding, or folding, drivers fell in love with the option to bring the great outdoors into their Beetles. For a while, the Volkswagen factory actually offered a sunroof conversion kit in addition to building cars with a ragtop built in.

During the 1980s, something

Hardtop sliding sunroofs were a popular option even back in the 1960s. You get the best of both worlds: clean lines and a bit of sunshine when you want it.

happened that made the ragtop trend take off for good. Original 21- and 23-window buses struck a nerve in car markets in Japan and Europe. Call it nostalgia or just backlash as drivers finally put their rearview-dangling disco balls away for good; the driving public turned back time to reach back to simpler days. They wanted old buses, but they also wanted some

more modern perks. The sunroof fit the bill perfectly.

However, if you've ever priced these buses (with or without the ragtop roof), you know that they don't come cheap. Especially these days, it's no longer shocking to see a beautifully restored 23-window bus sell for $300,000 at auction.

Faced with the choice of spending

With the prices of original ragtop buses going through the roof, even rides such as this 1967 are considered to be good cores for rebuilding.

Some cars came with ragtops from the factory. Some did not. With a good conversion, it is hard to tell the difference.

an arm and a leg on a ragtop-equipped bus or feeling trapped in a full-metal hardtop vehicle, Volkswagen enthusiasts became creative. Over the following decades, the demand for ragtop options has grown.

Demand Grows

But now the challenge for many is finding vehicles that are structurally sound enough to make the modification sensible. The demand is ever-growing as the supply of restoration-worthy rides continues to shrink. That supply-and-demand cycle has had a significant impact on the cost for drivers who want ragtop-equipped classics.

The marketplace made its wishes known. Do-it-yourself kits and done-for-you services offered by professionals, such as John Alba at Grumpy's Metal, answer that demand. In fact, it has never been easier to convert a vintage Dub's roof than it is now.

While there's no guarantee that a ragtop conversion will increase the value of a classic Volkswagen, there's a lot to be said for the personal enjoyment that a driver will receive from being able to open the roof and feel the breeze. So, if resale is your biggest concern, this may not be the modification for you.

Whether someone will pay more on the open market for a ragtop-equipped Beetle is up for debate. However, if you just want to enjoy your ride more, does that really matter? Make the conversion. Enjoy your ride. Let the resale value sort itself out when the time comes.

DIY versus Outsourcing

Two options are available to convert your hardtop into a ragtop: buy a kit to install the ragtop yourself or go to a reputable shop, such as Grumpy's Metal, to have it done for you. The results are essentially the same: you can peel back your roof to let in the sunshine. However, the methods are different.

With conversion kits, you receive all the sheet metal you need for the modification. You also get the assembly, handle, finish washers, rails, seals, and brackets—all the little pieces and parts needed to handle the project yourself, if you dare. If you find yourself immobilized and staring at the roof of your hardtop wondering whether the idea of cutting a hole in it means that you've lost your mind, you're in good company.

With proper instruction and patience and an excellent kit, you can absolutely make this customization. When done right, it will look great, function beautifully, and deliver pleasure that lasts for decades.

Use a flexible ruler. Go find the centerline of your roof, then use painter's tape to mark your centerline.

We prefer to use the ragtop frame as a guide for tracing the cut line. Trace the inner lip for your first cut.

Why Mess with Perfection?

The Beetle is nothing if not iconic. From Hollywood's *Herbie* to the avant-garde advertising of the *Mad Men* era, there's a certain emotional appeal that comes standard with the blandly named Type 1. In fact, there may be no other vehicle with such an enthusiastic following.

It's not at all uncommon for owners to siphon every cent of disposable income into making their Beetle better. With the addition of a ragtop roof, they amp up the enjoyment of getting in and taking their decades-old ride on a sunny drive to the beach, into the city, or up into the mountains.

If the thought of taking a Sawzall to your pristine Beetle roof doesn't leave you hyperventilating with fear, you're probably a brave do-it-yourselfer. This may be just the project for you, and you're in good company. For professionals with lots of practice, as long as they measure multiple times, they hardly bat an eye at the prospect of cutting the roof.

With John Alba's background in collision repair, he knows how hard it can be to take parts apart and put them back together over and over again. But that experience also made it clear that it was important to make getting the perfect fit easy. With that in mind, he makes his kits easy to install while minimizing the measurements that you need to take to get it to fit right. The kits ship worldwide and include all the parts you need. As he says, if you can weld, you can do this.

In fact, doing a ragtop conversion may be the perfect project for a VW enthusiast who takes pride in completing do-it-yourself projects. Further, this is an excellent project that you could do with your kids to pass along your passion for these cars while also giving them a taste for the satisfaction that comes with doing your own work.

After cutting the majority of the old roof out, set the new roof section in to dry fit. Then, mark and trim to fit as needed.

A pneumatic flanging tool will make things a lot easier. This will create a "shelf" for your panel to sit on in preparation for welding.

Protective equipment is a must while sewing with fire (also known as welding). A welding helmet and leathers will save you from UV exposure. When welding the ragtop section in place, run short beads to minimize warping. Do one section then move to another section, giving the first one time to cool.

Using a 6-inch dual-action (DA) pneumatic sander with 40-grit, prep your panel before filler. This is an important step for giving your subsurface "teeth." That will help the filler to adhere better.

Headliner

If you plan to replace your headliner, there is no better time than now to do it. In this case, rip the old headliner out before installing the ragtop kit. However, if you plan to retain your headliner, drop it out of the way during this installation. You can do so by removing the metal bows that support the headliner.

An alternative to dropping the headliner is also available if you have access to the specialized tools. You can cut through the roof sheet metal using a nibbler or shears without damaging the inner headliner. Once this hole is cut and the metal set aside, remove the metal headliner support bows.

Customize Your Bug with a Ragtop

Start by marking the cut lines on your roof according to the diagram or template included in your ragtop kit. Make a mark in the center of the roof, 6 inches back from windshield rubber molding. Make additional marks 8.75 inches in from each rain gutter above the rear edge of the door.

Set the frame onto your roof. The marks you just made should line up with the inside of the frame on the front and sides. Once the frame is in place and centered, draw a line completely around the inside edge of the frame. Remove the frame and set aside.

Out-size the hole using masking tape. The finished line for cutting purposes is 2 inches wider along the sides and 3/4 inch bigger on the front and rear edges. The final step in marking the hole is to add a radius to the corners. For this step, use any standard aerosol spray can for the proper curve.

Ready to Cut That Roof?

You'll see a set flange seam on the right. Put the flange into the metal using a flange tool. It creates a step lip that goes underneath the original roof after the cut to serve as an attachment point. That way, you don't have to butt-weld a triple-compound curve, which isn't nearly as fun as it sounds like it might be.

Now, your ragtop is prepped. It's been cut down to size and welded, and it's ready to install. But first things first. It's time to cut a giant hole in the roof of your car. Breathe.

To make the cut, use a reciprocating saw (Sawzall), a common jigsaw with a fine-tooth metal blade, or a cutoff wheel on a right-angle grinder.

Make the cut. The set of double lines is where the flange welds will go. The outer line is the outer piece of metal. The inner line is the flange relief drop.

Using a die grinder, create a slot in the roof for the saw blade by making a slice through the sheet metal along the cut line. You can also use a step drill.

Cut all of the way around the line and lift out the top. It is helpful to have someone on the inside of the vehicle to support the roof during this step.

Lift out the roof and discard.

Frame Installation

First, test fit the frame. It should drop freely into the hole. If not, trim the roof sheet metal as necessary. There are two ways to install this kit. The standard directions follow. However, if you choose, the frame can be installed from the underside of the roof sheet metal and molded in for the most original look.

Although the trim ring can be installed using a variety of fasteners, we recommend using urethane windshield glue to fasten the ring to the top of the car, thus eliminating any visible hardware. (We use 3M Superfast Windshield Urethane.) This type

Proper safety equipment is a must when welding. A proper, good-quality welding helmet will protect your retinas from being burned. Welding gloves protect your hands from thermal radiation.

After the roof section is welded in place, it is time for some light bodywork using kitty hair epoxy filler, a curve caster adjustable block, and some 80-grit file paper.

of adhesive allows plenty of working time and usually requires at least several hours to completely cure.

For faster drying time, you can use a metal-reinforced body filler like Evercoat Kitty Hair. While curing times are as fast as two minutes, the quick and proper placement of the frame onto the roof is essential with short working times.

Set the top frame in place on the car, being sure that the side with the latch slot and raised lip is toward the front of the car. Draw a line on the roof all the way around the frame.

Remove the frame and set aside. Place masking tape around the mark on the outside. This will prevent excess adhesive from getting on to the painted roof and avoid unnecessary cleanup time.

If you are using panel bond, here's how you'll proceed. When you are satisfied with trim placement, disassemble it again. You'll need to prepare the surface by scuffing it with 36- or 80-grit sandpaper. Apply enough adhesive to the underside of the part and clamp it in place on the car. Masking tape or clamps can help secure the part on the car until the adhesive has a chance to completely set up. Once the part is clamped in place, take the time now to clean up any excess adhesive before it cures.

If you prefer to weld your ragtop in, tack weld the frame in place. Aim for small beads (no more than 1/4 to 3/8 inch in length). Let the welds cool down. Move to another section about 7 to 8 inches away from your first weld to keep warpage to a minimum and repeat. Keep going around until you've welded the whole frame.

After all the welding is finished, it's time for a little bit of body filler just to level and smooth things out. A little bit of warpage is inevitable. You could metal-finish instead of using filler, but that's a rare skill.

Prime and paint the frame to match the body. Now, it's time to install the two long rails. You'll work from front to back.

More sanding! We have gone through three passes of filler and shot a high-build buff primer. We sand through the grits and add filler as needed as we sand it to be level.

With Grumpy's kit, you will receive all the hardware that is required. If you are restoring or using an OEM ragtop, they can provide replacement hardware for you.

Next, it's time to start working on the ragtop mechanism. The first piece to be installed is the headliner. This is way easier to do from outside of the car. You can either leave the frame finish as it is or finish and paint it the color of your car.

If you choose to leave it, run a clean bead of black silicone around the frame to prevent any water seepage. If you are going to paint the frame to match your car, you can either paint it now and silicone the edge or use a seam sealer around the frame first, and then paint it.

Once the glue is dry, cut out the center of the headliner to get it out of the way. Trim the headliner about 2 inches to the inside of the frame all the way around.

Headliner Installation

This is one of the trickier parts of the installation. Glue the front edge of the headliner to the bottom of the header bow. This is most easily done with the metal header bow cap not attached to the header bow.

The headliner hold-down strip (1/2-inch aluminum strip with pre-drilled holes) is installed on the top side of the headliner using sheet-metal screws. Once the conversion is done, this part will not show.

Now, the rear top hold-down (metal rear trim piece) can be preinstalled. Set the part in place on top of the frame along the rear. Drill a hole through the roof sheet metal using a small drill bit (1/8 inch).

Next, remove the part and ream out all of the guide holes just drilled with a 5/16-inch drill bit. This will allow for easier installation once the top is glued in place over the rear hold-down. Once the holes are drilled, attach black flathead machine screws through the hold-down using a self-locking nut.

Ragtop Installation

This step is the most crucial to a professional and proper-looking rag installation. When the sunroof is open, your new top will look great whether your installation is perfect or terrible, but when the top is closed, you are looking for a wrinkle-free, snug fit. This is a step that you may or may not want to

Ragtop Installation

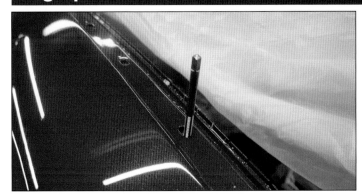

1 *You'll need to clean the threads of the capture nuts for the slide rail. Use an M 5.8 tap to chase the threads and clean up any paint on the inside of the threads.*

2 *Unbox the new or freshly chromed rails. You should have two longs and two shorts. Ours came from Grumpy's Metal.*

3 *Put the long rail into the channel first. Line up your capture nuts with the screws as you go. At this point, hand-tighten only. Start at one end and work your way down the rail.*

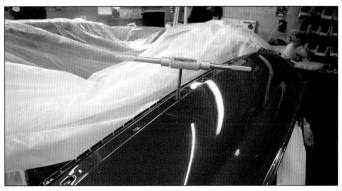

4 *After doing one side of the car, move to the other side. Once again, tap all of your capture nuts.*

Ragtop Installation *continued*

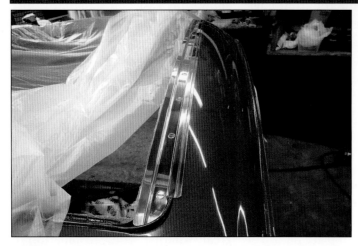

5 Install your second long rail. Once again, start from the windshield side and work your way backward to the rear.

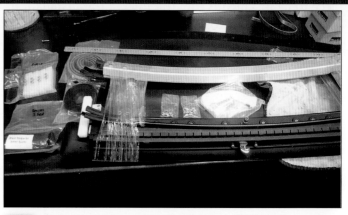

6 Unbox and inventory the frame, guide rails, seals, webbing, and hardware. Make sure you don't have any missing parts. Lay it all out to see clearly.

7 Attach the Teflon guide rails to the frame. There are two Phillips-head screws that go directly into a brass threaded insert in the Teflon slides.

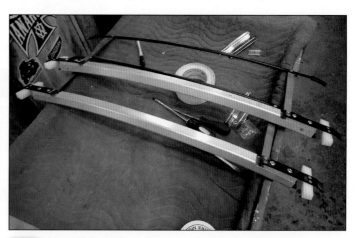

8 Install the other three in sequence. They are directional, meaning they need to go in in the right direction. Laying it all out in order first will make it easier to install.

9 Slide the header bow in first from the rear. There is a lower retaining slide that must fit underneath the rail. Push it all the way forward.

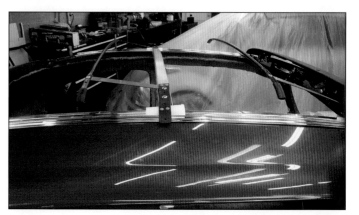

10 Next, slide the mid bow into place. Slide it up to about the halfway point. Make sure it moves freely once in place.

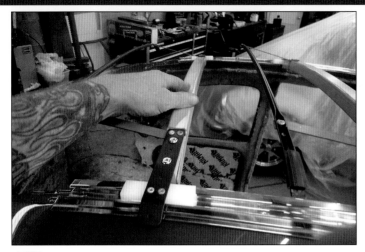

11 *Install the third and final bow. Do it the same way you installed the second one. Place it at the midway point on the track.*

12 *All three bows should be in the approximate position now before you install the headliner and canvas. At this time, apply a little bit of lithium grease to the track.*

13 *Next, install the short rear rail. This will ensure that everything is locked into place. You may need to do a little adjusting to get it all to line up 100 percent.*

14 *After everything is where you want it, it's time to tighten the rails. Go back and forth along the rail track, doing a quarter turn each. Repeat until it is all tightened.*

leave to an upholstery shop or convertible top shop.

If you choose to install the top yourself, use a spray contact cement. Pull and tape the top in place as shown in the series of photos. Mark the front and rear edges with chalk (the front edge of the header bow and the rear edge of the rear hold-down strip). These will serve as gluing reference points. The webbing is glued in place to the lower part of the header bow.

After the headliner is in, it's time to put the top on. Start by sliding the front cover around the upper header that you've already padded. Tuck it into place.

Glue it all down, then place the ends of the bows into the pockets sewn in the top. When the ragtop is completely installed, retain the original or new headliner using the black pinch molding supplied and trim off any excess headliner material.

After installing a layer of padding underneath the header bow, install the front part of the headliner. It clamps into a set of alligator clips on

Tools Required

Gather the following tools and equipment:
- Permanent marker
- Flexible tape measure
- Painter's tape
- Welder
- Grinder
- Flange tool
- Body fillers to finish your work

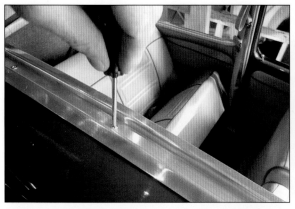

Three-fold ragtop long rails have nine screws that secure it to the captured nuts. Two-fold long rails have five per side.

If you are making a custom headliner, lay your material out on the roof before cutting. You have a curvature to pay attention to that will increase the length and width of the material needed.

the frame.

Finally, install the ribbed rubber seal along the front edge of the header bow. Then, after slipping the rear header bow in place, bolt it down from the inside.

Ragtop Maintenance

The top material is the same as would be used to manufacture any convertible top. Keep it clean by washing it with any mild car wash soap. Periodically, lubricate the aluminum rails using a spray silicone.

That's all that's involved in doing a ragtop conversion. As customization projects go, this one's fairly simple. Done right, the results far outweigh the expense and work that go into this modification. Just be patient and follow the instructions closely, or of course, you can always leave this and any other modifications to the professionals. Now, you'll understand the process they'll follow to do it.

The ragtop headliner is glued in place to the upper portions of the frame. Do a light tack first then close your headliner to make sure you don't have any sags or binding.

After slipping the outer canvas cover onto your ragtop, slide the ragtop to its closed position. This way you can get it to stretch out before you set your rear bow.

The rear bow has studs in it that drop through the back of the roof. They lock the headliner and ragtop section in place.

The last step is to install the short rails in the rear. There are two screws in each of the short rails. Apply a little silicone in the tracks and open and close the ragtop to lube the rails.

MISCELLANEOUS MODIFICATIONS

Some see classic Beetles as cars. Some see them as that and as a blank slate waiting for modifications that show off the owner's personality and style. So many opportunities exist for customization on a Bug, making it almost impossible to resist making "just one more" tweak.

Detailing every possible modification would require a book as thick as the old Yellow Pages phone directory that we used as a booster seat when we were kids. So, we've chosen some of the most common miscellaneous modifications we see.

Air-Conditioning

Imagine the wind in your hair, sunbeams glancing off your hood, and the gravelly purr of your Bug's engine serving as your ride-time soundtrack. What could be lovelier? Surprisingly, many drivers prefer having an arctic blast cool their cabin at the push of a button. Even more interestingly, the bulk of requests for air-conditioning upgrades we get at the shop come from convertible owners!

From the factory, Beetles came with heat exchangers only. That means the exhaust gas comes out

More horsepower doesn't have to mean going without heat. The heater boxes installed on this 1,914-cc engine will make even a cold day toasty warm.

of the engine and goes through the heater box. There's a heatsink covered in metal that directs the flow of cabin air forced out by the engine's cooling system. That heated air is directed back into the cabin to provide heat and to defrost your windshield.

The system works pretty well if your Beetle's seals are working correctly. However, it doesn't work well

before the engine comes up to operational temperature. So, for short rides, you'll arrive as cold as you left.

Air-Cooled Doesn't Mean Cool Air

While there may be no cooler car than a Beetle, there's usually no cabin cooling system in place. Air-conditioning was not available from the factory. However, many

No need for the old-style York compressors on modern air-conditioning. These compressors only pull about 3 hp off your engine.

The aftermarket vents fit snugly under this dash. They almost look like they came straight from the factory.

original owners opted either for a swamp cooler or for an actual air conditioner retrofit as a dealer option.

You may have seen the vintage advertisements proclaiming, "No Sweat: Cool it with a VW air conditioner." They were R-12 freon-based cooling systems, which are no longer available in the United States due to environmental concerns. So, while many Beetles are rolling around with these old air-conditioning systems, they're no longer serviceable. When the system runs out of freon, that's pretty much it. Before 1995, you could get it recharged, but not anymore, at least not legally or affordably.

Plus, since these systems were 30 to 40 years old, there are other challenges. While technically, you could retrofit these air conditioners to use currently legal and available cooling gases, there's still a problem. Their old York-style compressors were not as efficient as modern-day versions. So, they require more horsepower to drive them. Typically, the unit mounted to the engine bay, which is already a bit tight, so servicing them

and being able to reach other components became challenging.

Improved Efficiency

The best solution is to rip the old system out and replace it with a modern one. Not only will you be kinder to the environment while staying cool as you drive but you'll also draw less power from your engine. Modern air conditioners typically require only 1.25 to 4 hp to run. They usually use 134A refrigerant, which is more efficient and less harmful to the ozone layer.

If you're considering adding air-conditioning to your ride and also have a new engine in your upgrade plans, we recommend going with a heavier flywheel and crank pulley. It'll be easier to maintain your RPM and rotational mass. In plain English, if you have the air conditioner on and you take your foot off the accelerator, the engine will have trouble going back to idle until it catches up with itself. You want to keep your rotational mass going. Engines as small as 1,200 cc can bear this additional power load.

Physics lesson aside, if you want to make this modification to your Beetle, it's not particularly hard to do. You'll want to buy a classic Volkswagen-specific air-conditioning kit designed for your year. We've purchased a few from Gilmore Enterprises in Las Vegas and been pleased with the results.

Gilmore Enterprises makes kits for air-cooled Beetles from 1953 to

Two control knobs are all it takes. You can turn your system on and increase or decrease your blower speed.

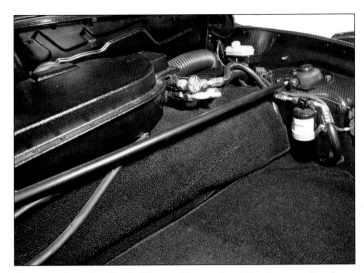

The condensing tank fits neatly against the inner wheel well. After all, you shouldn't have to sacrifice your trunk space.

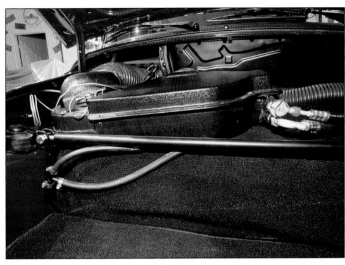

The air handler takes up a little more room in your trunk. But it fits neatly behind the dash, leaving you enough room to carry groceries too.

1970. You'll need to let them know what carburetor(s) your car has so they can build the right kit for you.

You won't need a shop full of tools, just a hole saw or two and an electric drill will do. You don't even have to brush up on your welding skills. The only cuts you'll make are five holes to accommodate four hoses for the air conditioner itself and one for the evaporator's drain hose. You can choose between an underdash or across-the-dash model.

TECH TIP
Check the Alternator

Before installing an air conditioner in your Beetle, check your alternator. You'll need peak performance to ensure your electrical system is up to the task. If you have charging issues, you should get them checked first.

Check your electrical system to ensure your grounding points are solid and free of rust and dirt.

Windshield Wipers

It's hard to imagine driving without windshield wipers. Follow a tractor-trailer on a rainy day, and you'd be one puddle splash away from driving blind. Yet, until 1961, that was just how it was. Do you want a clean windshield? Pull over onto the side of the road, whip out a rag and your preferred glass cleaner, and have at it.

As crazy as that sounds, it's equally hard to imagine how the Volkswagen factory engineers came up with their plan for how to wash the windshield while driving. In the old days, the spray mechanism functioned by pressurizing its fluid bottle by using air from the spare tire.

In its first iteration, the system consisted of a hand pump connected to a knob in the dash. The driver pushed the button to pump fluid onto the glass. Eventually, the factory figured out how to pressurize the fluid automatically without the muscle power of the driver.

Air to Spare

The setup was straightforward. The factory mounted the reservoir behind the spare (early models) or in the middle. Two hoses went into

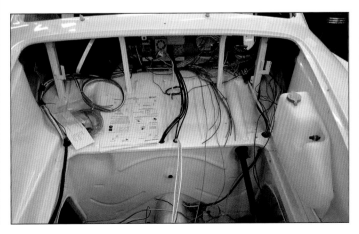

It's good to keep your wiring harness neat and tidy. It will be easier to troubleshoot later. Cloth wire wrap is a great replacement for the factory plastic.

Tools Required

Gather the following tools and equipment:

- Blast cabinet
- Powder coat kit
- Replacement nuts, washers, clips, grommets, ground strip, linkage rods, bushings, and pivot shafts
- High-temperature synthetic wheel bearing grease
- Sandpaper
- New brushes and springs
- Car battery
- Vise
- Superglue
- Round file

the reservoir. One connected to the washer nozzle on the hood in the middle of the windshield. The other connected to the spare tire with a valve stem.

All you had to do was overinflate your spare and you'd have clean windshields at your fingertips. It was elegant in its simplicity, as long as you kept your spare inflated adequately and didn't wind up with leaks in the hoses. As a safety mechanism, the system would not allow you to use so much air from your spare that you couldn't use your spare if needed.

If that setup sounds primitive, consider this. The early Beetle's wiper systems didn't have a self-parking function. That means that when you turned the wipers off, they'd stop in their tracks, staying exactly where they were rather than returning safely to their fair-weather resting places.

Some Beetle owners are still driving around like this! There is a bet-

ter way. There's an upgrade you can install that uses an electric pump and new tanks that will give you the power to clean your windshield as well as you could in a modern car. We highly recommend making this modernizing modification because not only is the old system archaic but also the rubber hoses of the original system break down and the fittings lose their sealing capability over time.

If the car has been converted from the 6-volt system to the 12-volt system, consider swapping the motor out for your wipers too. It's easy enough to do. Basically, an upgrade requires removing a lot of your underdash to get to the mechanism itself.

It's one of the first components to go in when we do a rebuild. It's always easier to install components at the point where they are most accessible rather than waiting until other components make reaching them a challenge.

You can get new wiper systems from a Volkswagen parts house. We've found that quality is hit or miss, though. Our preference is to have the original wiper mechanism restored, then fit it to a new motor and install new hoses.

Wiper Mechanism Restoration

Sure, you could buy a new one ready-made, but West Coast Wipers is the only specialist we know and trust to restore the originals with extreme care and attention to detail. West Coast Wipers takes the wiper assembly all the way apart, just the way we like it. Take every nut, bolt, wire off so you can make a brand-new, very old wiper assembly.

Wiper Restoration

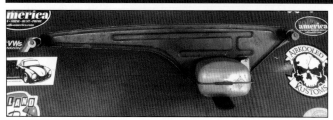

1 *Start by taking the wiper assembly entirely apart. The metal parts need to go through sandblasting to remove the paint. Send them out or buy a blast tank from a pawnshop or hardware store.*

Wiper Restoration *continued*

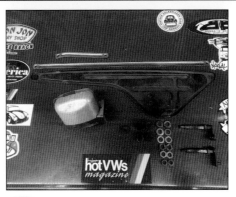

2 Once stripped, powder coat the frames and linkage rods glossy black. Take notes as you disassemble so you'll be able to put them back together.

3 Take the motor apart, cleaning and inspecting all components. You will need to replace any defective parts.

4 Replace all the hardware to install with new original equipment manufacturer (OEM) parts, including the nuts, washers, clips, grommets, ground strip, linkage rods, bushings, and pivot shafts.

5 Check for any binding of the linkage. Make sure it rotates and moves freely before installing the wiper motor.

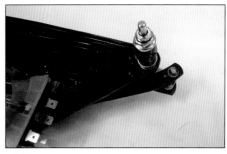

6 Put it on the bench and test after you've finished assembling. A little dab of molly lube on all moving components will help reduce the wear and give a longer service life.

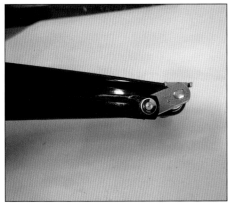

7 Install new bushings and springs. Double-check that the C-clips fit into the slots in the retaining groove.

8 A simple set of needle-nose pliers will make easy work of snapping the E-rings into place. Be careful not to bend the E-clip or you'll need a replacement.

9 Check both sides and all pin connectors. Manually turn over your linkage. Make sure that you still have smooth operation. Double-check the E-clips again before applying power.

Wiper Restoration *continued*

10 *Bench test the assembly by hooking it up to a car battery. Let it run for an hour just to be sure it is working correctly before mounting to the frame.*

11 *Service the gear case with new parts, grease, gasket contact terminals, and points. Wear gloves. This is the messiest part of the project.*

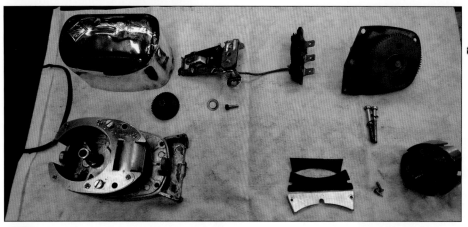

12 *Remove any dents in the aluminum covers. Sand and polish to get a smooth finish. You can paint, powder coat, or rechrome the cover depending on what you like.*

13 *This is a fully assembled frame with new shaft pivots, a ground strip, grommets, clips, washers, nuts, seals, and shaft caps. They keep the water from running down into the pivots.*

14 *It's always nice to have an OEM switch, wipers, and arms to go with a freshly rebuilt wiper motor assembly. Now, it's ready to reinstall and wire up. NOS beats new, in our book.*

By following this painstaking process to refurbish your wiper unit, you can get many years of trouble-free service from it.

Reinstalling Your Wiper Assembly

It's a reasonably straightforward process to reinstall your wiper assembly to your new wiper motor. Bolt the arm assembly to the motor, slip the shafts through the existing holes in the body, then bolt it all down.

Safari Windows

One of the quirkier looks out there for Beetles is the Safari wind-shield. Even the factory engineers would probably be surprised to see Beetles with this modification. Where Safari window buses with one open sort of look like they're winking at you, the Beetle's more like a one-eyed blink.

Safari windows were an option on the early split-window Volkswagen buses. While they look cool, the official purpose was to increase the airflow into the cabin. Buses are notoriously lacking in cabin airflow. Sure, the engines are air-cooled, but the passengers were anything but, without this option. After all, those side windows don't open very far.

Safari windows add a nice breeze to your cabin. They were a dealer add-on for early buses. Just watch out for bugs getting in your teeth.

On a Beetle, Safari windows add a certain cool factor, in every sense of the word. That's the upside, and it may outweigh any downside inherent to their design. There are a couple of downsides that the more pragmatic among us might count as deal breakers. Those include the potential for water intrusion in heavy rains, especially if you're driving fast enough to keep up with highway traffic. Plus, if a misguided flying insect has ever hit you at full speed, you know it's not a particularly pleasant experience. Therefore, it's probably not the safest idea in the world to drive with them open. In fact, that's a terrible idea, and you should never do it.

But leaving it open while parked? Even closed while parked? There may be no other small customization you can make to your Beetle

With Safari windows up, it's time for a cruise. You won't just look cool, you'll also enjoy a cooler ride with the added airflow.

that will make it stand out from the pack. Plus, what's a little rainwater between friends? Maintain your seals or carry a towel with you and remember that just as "beauty is pain," maybe "cool is wet."

Wipers with Safari Windows

If you're wondering how windshield wipers come into play with a windshield that's not permanently in its upright and locked position, you're probably getting serious about this option. There is a workaround.

Some Volkswagen parts suppliers

sell a rubber wiper blade rest, also affectionately known as a one-eyed duck. Coupled with a special Safari wiper shaft, this mechanism uncouples the wiper system, dropping it down so that it's not in the window itself.

Availability

Until fairly recently, it was a bit of a challenge to find Safari windows for Beetles. You'd see them here or there at car shows, but it took some hunting to find the parts. Now there are some options. Our favorite supplier is Jeremy Brooks of VW Loose-Nuts, who handcrafts Safari windows as a hobby. Because this isn't his full-time gig, there's a bit of a waiting list for buyers, but his handcrafted workmanship is well worth the wait.

This isn't a particularly hard modification project if you have basic welding skills and can put down a good bead. Technically, you

Fortunately, for Beetle owners, Type 1 Safari window kits are available. Just add your own glass, install, and enjoy the ride.

Jeremy at VW LooseNuts is manufacturing high-quality, limited-run Safari windows for Type 1s and Type 3s. He's also making rear Safaris for your Beetle's back end.

A full hardware kit is included. All the components are supplied, making installation on your Beetle a breeze. See what we did there? Just a little bit of welding is needed.

When installing Safari window hinges, go off the centerline of the roof and the centerline of the window. Check your reveal all the way around. Measure twice, drill once.

With the upper mounting hinge secured to the Beetle, all you have to do is screw it in place. The tap screws are included. Open and close your window to check for clearance.

could install Safari windows with tap screws where the pivot arms attach to the A-pillar. However, that's not the recommended method.

Installation

You can use your original windshield. If it's in poor condition, now would be a good time to replace it. Start by taking the Safari frame and making a mark on the car body where the screw holes go in. You'll make these marks on the hinge side.

Using the screws provided in the kit, attach the frame to the body. There are eight holes in the hinge.

Next, position the mounting plate on the A-pillar. It's approximately 2 inches from the bottom of the window frame. Tack weld the mounting plate to the A-pillar on both sides of the car. Then, install the arms over the bolt.

Double-check your fitment and the ease of movement. Make any adjustments needed until the mechanism opens and closes smoothly with no binding. When you're satisfied, weld the plates to the A-pillar.

Next, remove the Safari window frame. Carefully disassemble the two halves of the frame. There are two small screws on each side. Install the rubber seal on the outside of your windshield. Then, carefully reassemble your Safari frame and reinstall the windshield in your car.

If everything is operating smoothly, install the second seal that gets attached around the window frame. It will help prevent water from getting in. However, the best way to avoid a soggy ride is to keep your Beetle in a garage.

Sound System

Now, for some of us there is no better soundtrack for driving than listening to the distinctive hum of a Volkswagen engine. But others prefer that sound accompanied by music streaming through high-quality woofers and tweeters.

If you'd rather enjoy the sound of silence, you're driving the wrong car, but there is a radioless option. You can fit your dash with a radio delete panel and pretend it was never there.

From the factory, the Beetle's sound system was bare-bones basic.

There's not much room in a Beetle for a quality audio system. You can buy kicker panels that fit inside your footwell and will fit a small, high-quality speaker.

Generally, you'll find a Sapphire or Bosch sound system featuring a single speaker in the dashboard. Surround sound, it was not.

Most restoration clients whom we serve want at least a reasonably modern sound system with Bluetooth compatibility and good sound quality. It's a pretty standard upgrade, and it's one you can do rather easily.

Options

Essentially, there are two options for modifying your sound system. The first involves ripping the guts out of an original receiver and replacing what's in the housing with modern components to make it like new. The second is buying a modular kit specially manufactured to fit into various dashboard configurations. We use and like the modular kit Retro Sound makes.

Typically, it's a lot easier to make a sound system upgrade if you buy a pre-boxed sound system or a kit. That way, you know all the various components will play well together rather than working at cross-purposes. However, if you insist on piecing your system together, there's nothing stopping you.

Begin your research with brands you recognize. There is no shortage of companies out there making sound systems for cars; there is a huge range of quality, though. This is not the time to buy a sound sys-

tem off the shelf at a big box store. Do your research first.

Seek out products known to be high-quality. You can usually even talk with a real, live human at the brand's headquarters who can help you configure your ideal system. Ask lots of questions and make sure that what you buy will do exactly what you want it to.

Not all sound systems are alike or even meant to be. If you just want good, clean sound, you need different equipment than someone should buy if they want plain old "loud." Verify your amplifier's needs and capabilities. There are ratings to respect. You won't harm anything by buying the wrong equipment, but you can easily overpay and not get the results you wanted. Plan your whole system before you buy a single component.

Most manufacturers go out of their way to make sure customers can install their equipment. With some smart searching online, you can find detailed tutorials that will walk you through installing your particular equipment on your specific car. Bear in mind that the more complicated the system you choose is, the more math you'll have to do to get it installed correctly. If you use a fuse that's too small, you'll blow your wiring out, which is not fun.

As you shop, keep in mind that it's not as expensive as you might think

to get good sound quality. Just be sure to get equipment that matches your space. Buy one piece at a time if you need to. And remember, in a Beetle, a little bit of sound goes a long way. You don't need a massive system with three 10-inch subwoofers.

Wiring

Assuming you've upgraded your wiring harness to accommodate 12 volts rather than the original 6, and that you're using your original housing, installation is simple. Take notes and pictures as you remove your system. Then, do it all in reverse to put it all back in where it belongs.

But if you haven't taken that easy route, all is not lost. An extended automotive yoga session is in your near future. Brush up on your ability to read a wiring diagram and to use a voltmeter.

Start by removing the old radio so you can access the wiring behind it. You'll need to find a constant 12-volt wire in that tangle of wires. Double-check by turning your ignition on and off, then your headlights on and off while watching the voltmeter. If it stays at 12 volts, you've found your constant wire.

If you're working on a Beetle that no longer has a radio, you'll need to get a bit more resourceful because you probably don't have radio wiring, either. Instead, test the wiring connected to the ignition harness, fuse box, or cigarette lighter. Again, you need a constant 12 volts.

Any equipment you buy will come with specific installation instructions and a wiring diagram. A lot of the installation details will depend on the configuration you go with for your components. Be sure to plan your system before you start installing.

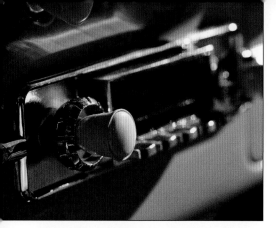

Retro Sound makes a classic-looking modern stereo that fits into your existing dash with a modular design. It even comes with period-correct trim plates.

As you work, be sure the power lines are fused and that every piece of equipment that's not a speaker has its own fuse. These fuses should be separate from the other components. Keep your signal and speaker lines away from your car's power lines, especially those with high current.

Once you install your system according to the manufacturer's instructions, test it. If the sound isn't everything you'd hoped, don't freak out. Even after installation, there is a lot of work to do to tune your system for your exact space. Imagine how different a sound system would sound in an SUV than it would in a Beetle.

You can imagine how many settings you might need to adjust to get the sound to match your space. Every good system comes with tons of paper documentation and videos you can follow to tune your system. Some are more technical and others are more user-friendly, so just keep looking until you find a guide you can use for your system.

It's also worth noting that all good sound equipment is thoroughly tested before it's shipped. If something's not working right, it's most likely because of user error. Don't hesitate to find someone who can help you if you get in over your head. It is far better to bring in an expert

than to blow your amp up because you wired something wrong.

Installation

Once you get past the wiring phase, installation is pretty straightforward if you bought one that was engineered to fit your dashboard. Not having to drill, cut, or otherwise modify your dash is a great reason to seek out a radio explicitly designed for your Beetle's year. Go this route, and you'll also get faceplates that match your car's year. The result will be a stock look as long as the system is turned off. The LED lights will give you away the moment you turn it on, though.

To install your radio, first, remove any knobs on it. With the knobs removed, locate the nuts and washers on the tuning shafts. Unscrew and remove them.

Remove the faceplate trim to expose the backing plate. Then, slide the radio into place from behind the dashboard, which is the only way it will fit into the hole. Make sure the radio is level and plumb, then reattach the faceplate. Reinstall the nuts and washers on the tuning shafts. Don't overtighten them.

Connect your radio to your wiring and enjoy some tunes.

Shifter

The upside of the unique VW shift pattern is, essentially, a double

Simple, classic, and timeless, it doesn't get any better than a short-throw shifter coupled with a Vintage Speed gear selector. You can refresh your old, worn-out knob with a stock-looking version, or you can go with an aftermarket version that suits your taste. Reverse is down and to the left!

Skulls may or may not be your thing, but there is a wide variety of aftermarket shift knobs that will fit your vintage shifter. Shift in whatever style suits you.

layer of security. Most kids these days do not know how to drive a manual transmission vehicle, but even if they can drive a stick, they probably won't find any of the gears if they take your VW on a joyride. Not that Volkswagen is the only manufacturer to feature this slanted shifting pattern.

Several other automakers use it, but it's not the norm overall. Another plus is that your odds of accidentally sliding into reverse are pretty low. You have to know where it is to find it. Plus, you have to press the shift-reverse lockout mechanism.

Beyond the whole shift pattern idiosyncrasy is an opportunity for further customization. Sure, you could keep the original stick shift in place and call it a day. But if you want something unique for your custom Beetle, you should consider upgrading to a sport shifter.

By upgrading to a performance shifter, you can improve the ease or speed of changing gears while also giving your Beetle a unique custom look. Entry-level aftermarket shifters are not particularly expensive, although as always, you will get what you pay for.

Installing it is a matter of removing two bolts, removing your old shifter, replacing it with the new one, and then screwing those two bolts back in. Easy.

You can keep it super simple and just swap out your shift knob. There are many aftermarket manufacturers making unique shift knobs. Or you can make your own from chains, bar taps, golf balls, cue balls, or nearly any object you can imagine. All you'd need to do is bore a hole into the object. Use epoxy to hold a capture nut in the hole. When the epoxy cures, simply screw the shift knob onto your shifter.

Window Tint

If you're cruising down the road in a classic Beetle, you don't need any help looking cool. But should you prefer not to get baked by the scorching sun or you just want to add an element of mystery to make people guess who's driving that cool-mobile, you might consider window tinting.

Especially suited for the "murdered out" black on black on black look, there's nothing that completes such a sinister look as well as tinted windows. In addition to the privacy afforded by tinting the windows, there's also the benefit of blocking UV rays. Not only does that protect you and everyone else with a window seat in your Bug but it will also help preserve your upholstery and other interior parts from the ravages of the sun.

When selecting your tint, adhere to the laws of your state. Individual states have different rules about shading. Buy the best quality you can afford for the best results.

Now, it's important to abide by your state's tinting laws. After all, it's far less cool to be sitting on the side of the road with blue and white lights flashing as you lower your too-darkly-tinted window and get a ticket. You'll need that ticket-paying money to buy more goodies for your ride.

If you plan to tint your own windows, triple-check that the film you buy is legal for your state. If you take your baby to a reputable tinting pro, the shop will explain the range of tints your state deems acceptable.

Tinting your windows is a relatively inexpensive upgrade, whether you do it yourself or take it to a professional shop. It's not a particularly daunting task, assuming you have a good eye for detail and the patience to complete the task the right way. Plus, unlike many modifications you might make, this one is easy enough to scrap and try again if needed.

Aside from the government's rules about tinting, you will have lots of choices when you start looking at the selection of films. You can choose from dyed film, metalized film, hybrid film, ceramic film, and carbon film.

Dyed Film

This is the most common type of window tint. Blocking up to 50 percent of the sun's rays, it works by absorbing the heat from the sunlight into your window glass. It's made up of a layer of dyed polyester film folded into a layer of adhesive on one side

and a scratch-resistant coating on the other side. It's applied to the inside of the windows and looks much darker from the outside than it does from the interior.

Dyed film is the most economical choice for tinting, but it's also not particularly long-lasting. The sun's UV rays will break it down over time, so you'll need to plan on replacing it. Of course, your mileage will vary, and how many years you get from your tint film depends on your location and how you store your car.

Metalized Film

This variation only reflects about 40 percent of the sun's rays, but it's got some other benefits too. Metalized tint film is composed of multiple layers. These layers offer some protection against having your window shatter. In a collision, the glass will still break, but it won't go flying everywhere.

This type of tinting film lasts quite a bit longer than dyed film because the pigment comes from microscopic metal particles. However, some drivers report issues with using their phone, GPS, and even their car's radio because the metal particles interfere with the signal.

Hybrid Film

Take all the benefits of dyed and metalized films, and you have the hybrid variation. It features multiple layers, including dyed film and metalized film, sandwiched between the hard outer coat and the adhesive side.

Tools Required

Gather the following tools and equipment:
- Heat gun
- Sharp utility knife
- Spray bottle with water
- Clean microfiber towel
- Squeegee
- Plastic card or scraper
- Straight razor

What you end up with is an economical option that lasts longer than dyed film and without the signal interference than regular metalized film. This type of film tends to come in lighter shades of tint rather than the blacked-out or mirror-like look.

Ceramic Film

This type took inspiration from metalized film, but instead of metal particles, it uses ceramic particles. Thus, there's no interference with signals when you're in the car. You still get up to 50 percent blocking power, but you also get really good visibility.

Ceramic film is significantly more costly than the other options. It can also be challenging to find in some locations. But the benefits include high UV ray resistance, less glare, less fading, and good shatter-resistance if your glass breaks. Plus, ceramic gives a beautiful matte look.

Carbon Film

Carbon film is how you go very, very dark. With a distinctive matte finish that lasts without fading, this tint blocks about 40 percent of the sun's rays. It's made with microscopic carbon particles. There's no metal in this type of tint, so your electronics will work just fine without interference.

The price tag may make your eyebrows go up, but as this type of tinting becomes more popular, the market may adjust. When you get into the higher-priced tinting options, the

idea of doing it yourself may become less attractive. It's one thing to scrap it and start over when you're using a more economical option. If you choose ceramic or carbon, and still want to do it yourself, just be extra patient and keep your investment in mind when you get tempted to take shortcuts.

You can buy film kits designed explicitly for Beetles. Look online, searching for your year. You will most likely still need to do a bit of trimming, but at least you'll be starting with film that's cut to the general shape and size of your windows.

Preparation

For the best results, take your time cleaning both sides of your glass. You want to remove any trace of grease, fingerprints, dust, and other debris. After cleaning, make sure the surface is completely dry.

Choose one window to work on first. Spray the exterior side of the glass with water. You'll fit the tint to the outside of the window but install it from the inside. The water will help hold the film in place so you can work with it and adjust as needed. Let the water do the work.

Start at the bottom of your window, then go to the sides. The top of the window goes last. Aim to get the tint edge within 1/4 inch of the window's edge. Use the knife to cut the film to fit your window. Anywhere there are recesses, press the film into the recess, then cut. Just follow the lines of your window frame to make your cuts precise. Round your corners slightly to minimize peeling and wrinkles.

You'll need to raise and lower the window to make sure you're covering all of the glass. When you're happy with the film's placement, use a heat gun on the outside of the window to

finalize its shape. The heat will make stretching and reshaping easy. Do not use the heat gun directly on the film.

As you size and shape each window's film, hang it to dry, noting which piece goes with which window. You can lay it flat to dry, but you will want to be sure the surface is super-clean, and then spray it with water to keep the film from sticking.

Tint Film Installation

Now, it's time to apply the film to your windows. First, remove the adhesive backing. Spray that side of the film with water. By keeping it slightly wet, you'll be able to adjust the film on the glass to get it to fit just right.

When you have the film in position, press it onto the interior side of the window. Start in the middle of the window and work your way outward. The idea is to push all the air out from under the film. Use your plastic card or scraper to push the film into the corners.

If the film starts to harden before you're finished, shoot the outside of the glass with the heat gun to keep it pliable enough to work with again. If your edges are a little rough, smooth them with the metal file. When you work on the front and rear windshields, you may find it easier to work from one side of the car to the other rather than from the middle to the outer edges.

Curing Time

Your tinting film needs time to cure. Do not roll your windows down or use your wipers for two to four days. Check the film manufacturer's instructions to find out what time frame and temperature range they recommend.